Building *on the* Strengths *of* Students *with* Special Needs

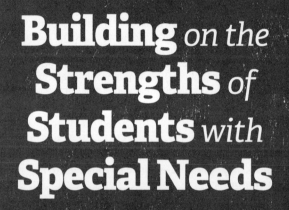

Building on the Strengths of Students with Special Needs

How to Move Beyond Disability Labels in the Classroom

TOBY KARTEN

ASCD

ALEXANDRIA, VIRGINIA

1703 N. Beauregard St. • Alexandria, VA 22311-1714 USA
Phone: 800-933-2723 or 703-578-9600 • Fax: 703-575-5400
Website: www.ascd.org • E-mail: member@ascd.org
Author guidelines: www.ascd.org/write

Deborah S. Delisle, *Executive Director;* Robert D. Clouse, *Managing Director, Digital Content & Publications;* Stefani Roth, *Publisher;* Genny Ostertag, *Director, Content Acquisitions;* Allison Scott, *Acquisitions Editor;* Julie Houtz, *Director, Book Editing & Production;* Jamie Greene, *Editor;* Donald Ely, *Graphic Designer;* Mike Kalyan, *Director, Production Services;* Kelly Marshall, *Senior Production Specialist;* Keith Demmons, *Production Designer*

PAPERBACK ISBN: 978-1-4166-2357-1   ASCD product #117023   n3/17
PDF E-BOOK ISBN: 978-1-4166-2359-5; see Books in Print for other formats.
Quantity discounts are available: e-mail programteam@ascd.org or call 800-933-2723, ext. 5773, or 703-575-5773. For desk copies, go to www.ascd.org/deskcopy.

Library of Congress Cataloging-in-Publication Data

Names: Karten, Toby J., author.
Title: Building on the strengths of students with special needs : how to move
   beyond disability labels in the classroom / Toby J. Karten.
Description: Alexandria, Virginia : ASCD, [2017] | Includes bibliographical
   references and index.
Identifiers: LCCN 2016052094 (print) | LCCN 2017004855 (ebook)
   ISBN 9781416623571 (pbk.) | ISBN 9781416623595 (PDF) | ISBN 9781416623601 (EPUB)
Subjects: LCSH: Children with disabilities--Education. | Mainstreaming in
   education.
Classification: LCC LC4015 .K35 2017 (print) | LCC LC4015 (ebook) | DDC
   371.9--dc23
LC record available at https://lccn.loc.gov/2016052094

26 25 24 23 22 21 20 19 18 17   1 2 3 4 5 6 7 8 9 10 11 12

Building *on the* **Strengths** *of* **Students** *with* **Special Needs**

How to Move Beyond Disability Labels in the Classroom

Introduction

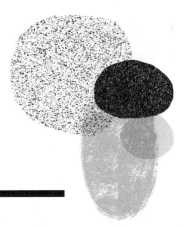

Building on the Strengths of Students with Special Needs describes the characteristics and strengths of specific disabilities as well as inclusion strategies to implement in your classrooms. Inclusive curriculum scenarios for younger learners and secondary students in elementary, middle, and high schools are included. Each chapter highlights a specific disability, but it is essential to note that students are individuals, regardless of whether they share a disability label. In addition, characteristics of certain disabilities often overlap with one another. In other words, a student who is classified with a specific learning disability may also have attention and social differences. A student with dyslexia may demonstrate signs of ADHD, whereas a student with an intellectual disability may also have a speech or language difference. Therefore, the classroom inclusion strategies in this book are not restricted to their respective chapters.

Also typical is a combination of symptoms and characteristics with a range of severity. All human beings, whether they have a disability or not, exist on a spectrum with a profile of strengths and weaknesses. A student with dyslexia may have weaknesses in reading and writing skills yet also exhibit strengths that need to be recognized and nurtured. Perhaps he or she is a wonderful musician or artist, in which case you provide opportunities to create a rap or folk song, collage, or digital presentation about a novel. A student with emotional disturbance may be an excellent writer, or a student with a hearing impairment may have an affinity for science. The bottom line is that teachers and other staff can ease the classroom struggles a student may have by capitalizing on his or her stronger skills, interests, and abilities and by valuing who the student is with responsive, appropriate inclusion interventions. Our aim is to circumvent a disability label from defining that student.

My first year of teaching, back in 1976, was in a private school in a Brooklyn brownstone. The population of learners was diverse. The students had varying socioeconomic levels, ethnicities, and cognitive, communicative, sensory, and physical abilities. Some carried the labels of Tourette's, scoliosis, cerebral palsy, autism, emotional disturbance, and learning disability. Some were classified with terms that are no longer used today, such as *mental retardation* (now known as intellectual disability) and *minimal brain dysfunction* (generally referred to today as attention deficit hyperactivity disorder, or ADHD).

When I handed one student any two writing implements—whether it was two crayons, two pencils, or two markers—he would shout out "Sword fight!" and duel with himself. I had a student who swore a lot, another who only wrote capital letters, and yet another who had echolalia and would repeat what was said to him or what he heard from television commercials. Some students spoke English, some used sign language, and some spoke languages other than English as their primary language. Some learners entered the classroom with a lovely packed lunch, some had no lunch, and some came off the bus with physical and emotional bumps and bruises.

Even though the public school system decided that these learners were best educated in a separate environment—that was not their neighborhood school—I never viewed any of these students as broken or unable to learn. All of them shared a few commonalities: they were in the same school, in the same class, and had me as their teacher. As a young new educator, I eagerly and enthusiastically figured out how to teach and reach each student. Some of the methods were conventional, and some were unconventional at the time. We recited rhyming words, read books, wrote captions for pictures in magazines, created stories, wrote in journals, solved math word problems, and completed research reports. We also traveled the New York City transit system to visit museums, took nature walks, spent time in local parks, bought items in bodegas, rode through a car wash, and visited Chinatown.

Along with direct-skill, whole-class instruction, and individualized learning, I provided my students with more real-life experiences (infused with academic and functional skills) so they could be part of their community and city. The school was not a microcosm of the world, since it had learners with atypical behavior and learning characteristics that did not emulate those of their age-level peers. These students had what others viewed as obstacles, but I viewed their differences as educational challenges that were mine—not theirs. It was *my* challenge to teach them. And, happily, I did.

Years later, I taught learners in both public and private schools in several states; coached special and general educators; collaborated with administrators in school districts; prepared university students to become educators; and presented professional development sessions in several different countries. Having met so many diverse learners, I realize that a student's label is inconsequential. A label may be legislatively required to ensure that a student receives services, but that label does not offer insights into his or her likes, dislikes, interests, strengths, and potential.

The infancy of groundbreaking legislation for students with disabilities coincided with my preservice years in special education. During my junior year in college, Public Law 94-142, the Education for All Handicapped Children Act (EHA), was passed. The year was 1975, more than four decades ago. This landmark legislation has since been amended, improved, reinterpreted, and renamed the Individuals with Disabilities Education Act (IDEA). Prior to 1975, students with disabilities were often not included in classes or schools with nondisabled peers. The mindset was that students with learning, attention, memory, emotional, social, behavioral, communicative, developmental, and physical differences were not on par with students who were considered to be *typical* learners. Limited access, lower expectations, and negative stereotypical thoughts yielded a generation of learners who often dropped out of school (Vaughn, Danielson, Zumeta, & Holheide, 2015).

Today, as a requirement of IDEA, each student who receives special education services has his or her learning needs identified in a legal document known as an individualized education program (IEP). The contents of an IEP include, but are not limited to, a statement of the learner's present level of academic achievement and functional performance (PLAAFP), learning goals, and related services provided, such as occupational and/or physical therapy, psychological, audiological, vision, orientation and mobility, and speech and language services and supports. The IEP also outlines the rationale for the placement, the extent of participation in the general education classroom, types and length of time for the services and supports provided, the specific location of the delivery of services, and necessary accommodations and modifications (e.g., additional time on tests; closer proximity; visual, auditory, kinesthetic, tactile presentations). As necessitated, transitional services are planned for in a student's IEP, and extended school year (ESY) services—if required—are also specified if it is determined that the learner will regress over the summer months.

The *I* in IEP mandates that the goals and instructional decisions are individualized ones—never based on a school district's availability of services but linked to a student's determined current level of performance. The goals are also measurable, designed to involve the student in the general education curriculum to the maximum extent appropriate. The general education classroom is considered to be the least restrictive environment (LRE), with other placements on a continuum from least restrictive to most restrictive. This continuum ranges from a general education classroom with supplementary aids and services to a general education classroom with a coteacher and/or consultative services. These services could also include a combination of in-class and pull-out services with a resource teacher, services provided in a self-contained special classroom, placement in a special school or through homebound or hospital instruction, or separate placement in a residential school or setting. Decisions are based on each student's unique needs and levels, with instruction that acknowledges each learner's challenges and strengths.

IDEA's intent is to offer each learner with a disability a free and appropriate public education (FAPE) with continuous monitoring and communication of progress achieved toward outlined learning goals. IEP teams include school staff, families, invited guests who have information to contribute, and the learner if he or she is willing and able to participate in the process. A student is evaluated to determine his or her level of functioning. There are 13 disability classifications under IDEA, which include autism, visual impairment (including blindness), deafness, deaf-blindness, hearing impairment, specific-learning disability, emotional disturbance, intellectual disability, multiple disabilities, orthopedic impairment, traumatic brain injury, speech or language impairment, and other health impairment. Developmental delays include learners from birth to age 3 and children from ages 3 to 9. Children with developmental delays are identified by each state in areas of development that include cognitive, physical, social, emotional, communicative, and adaptive-behavior.

If a child does not qualify for services under IDEA, then he or she may be eligible for services under what is referred to as a 504 plan. Section 504 of the Rehabilitation Act of 1973 is intended to eliminate discrimination against students with disabilities, regardless of the nature or severity of a disability (U.S. Department of Education, Office of Civil Rights, 2015). As an example, a learner with attention deficit hyperactivity disorder may not qualify under other health impairment (OHI) under IDEA but instead receives educational services with a 504 plan. A student who receives services under a 504 plan is determined to have a physical or mental impairment that substantially limits one or more major life activities (e.g., breathing, walking, seeing, hearing, speaking, learning, working). Services and placements include, but are not limited to, general education classrooms with supplementary supports and/or the provision of special education services in a separate setting. As with an IEP, a 504 plan is individually based and collaboratively planned, monitored, and evaluated to determine the location and appropriateness of services. Funding differs, but services are always individually based.

Another piece of legislation, the Americans with Disabilities Act (ADA), was first enacted in 1990 to prohibit discrimination against people with disabilities—in reference to employment, public accommodations (including school settings), commercial facilities, and access to transportation. Like IDEA and Section 504, ADA has been amended over the years to improve services. ADA broadened the definition of *disability* in the latest amendments to prohibit discrimination and ensure equal opportunities for people with disabilities. School examples include a bathroom or classroom door widened to permit access for a student in a wheelchair, note takers provided for learners who have difficulty writing, sign language interpreters provided at a school play, and other classroom and extracurricular supports as necessitated. Children who qualify for IDEA eligibility criteria are also protected by Section 504 and ADA, with identified impairments.

Even though legislation protects the rights of learners with disabilities, both within and outside school settings, diversity is often viewed through different lenses. Thankfully, much progress has occurred since policies such as sterilization, institutionalization, and exclusion of people with differences went into effect. The so-called ugly laws (Schweik, 2011), which prohibited deformed—or what was considered "unsightly"—people to be seen in public in some locations of the United States, gave birth to substantial civil rights legislation. However, some disabilities today are viewed through more positive lenses and given more acceptance than others. For example, there is still a lack of information and a stigma for students within certain disability categories. Before brain research revealed that differences such as dyslexia and ADHD were not willful but had brain etiology, some people viewed learners with these labels as lazy or deliberately defiant.

The characteristics and effective classroom strategies that capitalize on the strengths that a student with a difference, such as emotional disturbance or deafness, possesses are often misunderstood. Some categories of disability are more tolerated than others considered "hidden" or less visible to the eye. As examples, a staff member would never ask a student seated in a wheelchair to just stand up and walk like everyone else does, a student who is blind to see, or a student who is deaf to listen, so why would a student with an emotional disturbance be asked to behave differently or a student with a specific learning disability be asked to perform classroom expectations without the necessary supports and scaffolding? A student with a physical disability may require a wheelchair or braces, whereas a student with a visual impairment will need magnified pages and digital recordings. Accordingly, students with learning and behavioral disabilities also require specific evidence-based strategies to succeed in school settings. The definition of *diversity* has greatly widened in today's classroom to view a disability as a characteristic—not a deviance to be hidden or erased. The definition of *normal* often indicates that a problem exists within a student instead of expecting or requiring educational contexts to be more responsive (Moore, 2013).

All students are exceptional, whether or not they have a label. As stated throughout this book, each child is different. Reinforcement, motivation, modeling, collaborative planning, and scaffolding help educators provide learners of all ability levels with opportunities to achieve greater academic, social, emotional, and behavioral goals. No student has a monopoly on being a learner, and no learner is perfect. Special and general education teachers collaborate to intervene with strategies that are tailored to personalize instruction. The Every Student Succeeds Act (ESSA) speaks about challenging and personalizing student learning. This includes providing diverse supports, interventions, and assessments that reveal and measure individual growth. Each child is born as a unique individual that personalized education addresses, whether or not a student has an IEP or an assigned label. ESSA describes a competency-based approach that values not only summative assessments but also formative and performance-based ones.

Learning is a process. As a novice yoga practitioner, I can finally *almost* maintain a tree pose for a full minute without toppling over—after more than a year of classes. A yoga instructor pointed out that we are each at a different stage of development and that yoga includes a mind-body connection. She poignantly told the class not to measure our worth by what others are doing but to praise ourselves for being part of the class—each of us cherishing our efforts and unique levels of participation.

Change is an evolutionary process. Learn how to value the plan, stay the course, and weigh options. Not every day is a perfect one—nor does the perfect child or the perfect lesson plan exist. We are all malleable, inclusive educational partners on the journey together—whether we are considered gifted, autistic, twice-exceptional, or are identified as having a learning, speech/language, or emotional disability. We require professional knowledge, a plan to move forward, and the fortitude and patience to stay the course. It is okay to mess up, but it is *not* okay to stay that way. Most important, a positive attitude and a belief that all students are capable of achieving self-efficacy and making strides alongside their peers are critical.

I once stopped a lesson when one of my students was overly concerned with a comment that another student made to him and took personal offense. No matter what I said or did, he would not let it go. I then wrote in large letters on the board, "BIG DEAL, SO WHAT—NOW WHAT?" Suddenly, I had the attention of the whole class, and the student paused to think. We all need to pause to think and then plan our next move. We use data to guide our decisions, regardless of the perceived obstacles or hurdles presented. Always keep the inclusive wheels turning.

This book maintains that diversity is first identified and then embraced to honor learner differences with the appropriate systematic instruction. Students should never be viewed as failures but as learners who require the effective strategies that capitalize on and strengthen their levels of performance. *Typical* instruction needs to match the diversity of *atypical* learners, without viewing a disability as being on a lower rung of the educational ladder.

Points to emphasize in your classroom include the following:

- Each student is different!
- Reinforcement should be consistent, realistic, and enthusiastic.

- Motivators can be both extrinsic and intrinsic.
- Desired responses need to be modeled.
- Appropriate collaborative planning, pacing, and step-by-step scaffolding increase skill sets.
- Academic, social, emotional, and behavioral objectives are often intertwined.
- Data should drive instructional decisions.
- Classroom organization includes multitiered systems of support (MTSS).
- Accountability includes staff, students, and families.
- Every moment of the day is an educational one!

References

Americans with Disabilities Act of 1990 and Revised ADA Regulations Implementing Title II and Title III, 2010 ADA Regulations. Available: www.ada.gov/2010_regs.htm

Moore, B. (2013). *Understanding the ideology of normal: Making visible the ways in which educators think about students who seem different.* ProQuest LLC, Ph.D. dissertation, University of Colorado at Boulder.

Schweik, S. (2011). Kicked to the curb: Ugly law then and now. *Harvard Civil Rights-Civil Liberties Law Review Amicus, 46,* 1–16.

U.S. Department of Education, Office of Civil Rights. (2015). *Protecting students with Disabilities.* Available: http://www2.ed.gov/about/offices/list/ocr/504faq.html

1

Students with Dyslexia and Other Reading Differences

The Possible Whys

Brain scans indicate that people with dyslexia have differences in a part of the brain called the corpus callosum. The corpus callosum is composed of nerve cells that connect and transport information and messages back and forth from the left and the right sides of the brain. Balance and communication between the two sides yields optimum learning. Each side—or hemisphere—is programmed to perform different functions. The left side of the brain sees things from their constituent parts to the whole. Someone who is predominately left brained notices the details before seeing the whole. For example, they may gaze at the night sky and focus on each star rather than see the big picture of the sky.

As related to reading, the left side logically lines things up in a structured manner to

- Match letters with sounds.
- Separate a word into its constituent sounds.
- Decipher grammar and syntax.

By contrast, the right side (often referred to as the creative part of the brain) sees words in their entirety as pictures, shapes, and patterns (not a mixture of individual sounds).

The characteristics of the right side of the brain are collectively analogous to gazing at the night sky and not seeing individual stars or viewing the ocean without seeing the crests of the waves. Words are composed of letters that make discrete sounds, but a student with dyslexia has difficulties understanding these individual phonemes. Faulty signals between the two sides of the brain result in an inability to decipher and interpret written language. Dyslexia tends to run in families, with genetic implications evidenced (Lyon, Shaywitz, & Shaywitz, 2003; Siegel, 2006; Wagner & Torgesen, 1987).

Characteristics and Strengths

Dyslexia has cognitive correlates underlying reading that affect phonological and orthographic processing, rapid automatic naming (RAN), processing speed, working memory, attention, and executive function (State of New Jersey Department of Education, n.d.). Simply put, phonological processing affects understanding, learning, and remembering how to associate sounds with the letters that make up the word and how to break up a word into its discrete sounds. Students with orthographic processing differences have difficulties learning how to form or copy letters and remembering sight words. Although letter reversals may be a characteristic of dyslexia, it is only a slice of the orthographic processing difference that a student with dyslexia experiences. At times, students with dyslexia confuse similar-looking letters and words and have difficulties encoding (spelling) and decoding (reading) words. Even though these characteristics are evidenced, a student with dyslexia is often able to tap into stronger modalities. Learners can decipher words through appropriate multisensory instruction such as touching raised letters to increase spelling skills, snapping or clapping out each syllable in a word to pronounce it, listening to a digital recording of a book, recording a lecture, illustrating concepts as a demonstration of comprehension, and using syllabication to break up more difficult vocabulary presented in an algebra, science, or history text.

Warning signs of dyslexia include—but are not limited to—differences in language, reading, writing, and social-emotional domains (National Center for Learning Disabilities, 2015). Students may experience inaccurate or nonfluent word recognition. They may also be good word memorizers, but they're not learners who have cracked the phonetic code and "own" the individual sound-symbol connections they see and hear. Some learners with dyslexia get by in the early grades because they are excellent memorizers and can retrieve a file of sight words that they have stored in their brains. Beginning in kindergarten and 1st grade, these students exhibit low levels of phonemic awareness and cannot take apart the individual sounds that make up words. They also exhibit similar deficits with respect to phonics and an inability to learn the unique sounds associated with letters. Other types of reading disabilities include specific difficulties with reading comprehension and processing speed (i.e., reading fluency). Generally, students with dyslexia do not read with automaticity.

Dyslexia affects reading from the early grades, and primary symptoms include complications with the following literacy skills (International Dyslexia Association, Professional Standards and Practices Committee, 2010):

- Word recognition
- Spelling
- Reading fluency
- Comprehension
- Written expression

People with dyslexia may also display characteristics of other differences or disorders, which is referred to as comorbidity (Germanò, Gagliano, & Curatolo, 2010; Snowling, 2012). Ben Foss, an entrepreneur, advocate, and author of *The Dyslexia Empowerment Plan*, explains comorbidity in relation to his dyslexia:

> Everyone in Dyslexia carries a passport that allows easy entry into a number of bordering countries, including the nations of Dyscalculia, Dysgraphia, and ADHD, to name some of the major ones. In my view, we are all "in the club"—my catchphrase for the broad family of people who experience the non-obvious disabilities generally housed under the umbrella of "specific learning disabilities" . . . holding dual citizenship with each one of these. (Foss, 2013, p. xi)

This quote sheds light on the fact that dyslexia interventions need to be comprehensive ones that address deficits in reading, writing, mathematics, and attention, along with behavioral, emotional, and social domains. As an example, learners with dyslexia who evidence signs of dysgraphia experience weaker writing skills. These learners may be unable to accurately copy, organize, or read class notes. To capitalize on stronger modalities, offer these students alternative ways to capture information, such as a digital pen that records information, graphic organizers, or peer scribers. A student with a reading and math difference such as dyscalculia or an attention difference such as ADHD requires math and behavioral strategies as well as reading interventions. He or she benefits from a digital version of a math lesson to stop and then play back, as well as feedback for time on task, effort given toward mastery, and recognition of positive class participation. Acknowledgment of reading strides achieved and progress toward IEP goals is essential.

Even though a learner with dyslexia often has difficulty decoding and encoding words and formulating written expressions, he or she may be highly creative, possess strong personal skills, and have an excellent oral vocabulary. Nurturing these strengths with the appropriate classroom interventions is essential (Yale Center for Dyslexia and Creativity, n.d.). For example, instruction and assessments are not exclusive to verbal and written ones, but they also include debates, cooperative learning projects, and multimodal engagements. Using technology to represent, access, and demonstrate knowledge minimizes some of the weaker characteristics that often challenge learners with dyslexia. The strategies in this chapter (and subsequent ones) are not only instructional but also have practical classroom, school, and "real-life" applications.

Classroom Implications

School staff require training in specific ways to identify students who show signs of dyslexia at early ages before their language processing difficulties spiral and multiply into additional academic, social, emotional, and behavioral domains. These concerns also need to be addressed before the reading demands increase. In addition, students who have advanced a grade—being socially promoted but are still educationally underserved—should be recognized as learners who require specific strategies to close their reading gaps.

School staff members need to collaborate effectively to intervene with strategies and interventions. As examples, a physical education, art, music, science, math, or social studies teacher needs to provide appropriate scaffolding. This includes interventions that do not permit a student's reading difficulties to interfere with successes (e.g., access to the content in each discipline and an ability to interpret the directions on a worksheet or an assessment, follow safety procedures in a science lab or gymnasium, and effectively answer a document-based question in social studies). Students should not be penalized for a diagnosed difficulty but instead offered multiple avenues of access, such as digital text, alternative reading levels of the same content, math word problems read aloud, science lab procedures verbally communicated, and increased visuals across the disciplines.

The primary characteristics of dyslexia include difficulty reading real words in isolation, decoding nonsense words, spelling, and accurate oral reading. The secondary consequences of dyslexia include but are not limited to inconsistencies in schoolwork with lower levels of reading comprehension and writing skills, and increased distractibility (Moats & Dakin, 2008). The secondary consequences often lead to frustration with school assignments and anxiety when students are required to read in front of peers (Torgesen, Foorman, & Wagner, 2007). Since staff members and students with dyslexia do not always understand the disability, blame is often incorrectly applied to an individual's lack of effort. A student with dyslexia requires the appropriate academic and behavioral interventions that honor his or her strengths. Weaknesses need to be remediated—not highlighted or magnified. It is vital to note that the educational practices for literacy instruction are never exclusively limited to students who have reading goals listed in IEPs or 504 plans but are applicable to all students. Learners across skill sets and grades benefit from systematic instruction that honors diverse interests and levels. Read on for more specific strategies.

Inclusion Strategies

➲ Identify, Screen, and Individualize

Because students with dyslexia exhibit different characteristics, it is imperative that accurate screening continually drives individualized interventions. This includes informal phonics inventories as well as formal evaluations by trained professionals who determine skills through rapid naming of letters and sounds, identification of real and nonsense words, and activities around vocabulary, phonemic segmentation, spelling, verbal fluency, rhyming, and passage interpretation. Early literacy skills include—but are not limited to—knowing the sounds and names of letters, sequencing letters and numbers, and speaking in simple sentences. Levels of performance are screened with oral reading tests, checklists, parent interviews, nonverbal reasoning assessments, written assessments, and more. Alphabetic principles and phonemic awareness skills are often addressed as early as preschool. Screening for phonological awareness, rapid naming and memory begins in kindergarten, and testing in 1st grade includes word reading, decoding, and spelling. All learners across the grade levels who struggle need to be screened so they receive the appropriate instruction. Older learners also require screening, since high-quality literacy instruction is appropriate for high school and beyond (Alliance for Excellent Education, 2006).

➲ Appropriately Tier Literacy Instruction

Educators also need to infuse multitiered systems of support (MTSS). In MTSS models, learners receive literacy interventions in tiers. There is no template for tiered literacy instruction since it is generated by the data. For example, a model with three tiers has all learners participating in the first tier: core literacy instruction. This core instruction includes an entire class learning together with a combination of direct instruction and literacy instruction in smaller cooperative groups. Based on progress monitoring, supplementary literacy instruction is provided to secondary groups of students who require additional literacy practice with skills for fluency, automaticity, and mastery. As indicated by formal and informal literacy assessments, more intensive instruction is given to a third tier with small-group or individualized instruction provided.

When students read slowly, their comprehension is negatively affected. They read each word so slowly that they consequently struggle to determine text meaning; they laboriously read letters and words, which interferes with comprehension flow and text meaning. Students who try to decode irregular sight words inappropriately (e.g., *people, could, whose*) lose the gist of a passage read. When this happens, it's important to increase oral and shared readings with the whole class, small groups, and individual students as appropriate. Interventions that offer increased guided oral reading assist with fluency. This includes learners becoming more strategic with both oral and silent reads (e.g., interest-related readings on students' instructional level and modeling) (Guerin & Murphy, 2015).

Strategies for fluency also change as students advance through the elementary grades. As learners advance, their reading fluency is affected by several factors, including the display of different skill sets and frustrations. The fluency of 1st graders is more dependent on listening skills, whereas reading fluency and comprehension play a larger role in grades 2–4 (Kim & Wagner, 2015).

Alternatively, for older students who require basic reading skills, present age- and level-appropriate readings with motivating content and appropriate vocabulary that is not insulting to a learner's age. Even though a secondary student may be reading at a primary level of instruction, do not offer juvenile text. For example, if short vowel sound instruction is required, then replace a sentence such as *The cap is on the cat* with a more sophisticated sentence such as *The raft capsized on Saturday*. There is no need for staff to rewrite texts since many publishers and online sites provide high-interest, lower-level text for older learners. Online sites such as Smithsonian's Tween Tribune and Newsela provide the same content for nonfiction articles on multiple Lexile levels. A site such as Starfall may have an excellent video on how to chunk a word for a 2nd grader, but it would be an inappropriate choice for a secondary-level student who requires the same skills. Benchmark, Steck-Vaughn, Perfection Learning, Curriculum Associates, High Noon, and Saddlebrook are just a few of the many publishing sources to explore. In other words, offer age-appropriate reading selections and tools that entice readers to decode and encode words. High-interest topics such as fashion, music, and sports and alternative presentations such as tweets, texts, and cooperative projects are viable secondary engagements.

◉ Structure, Monitor, and Communicate

Direct, structured, and systematic instruction includes teaching phonemic awareness; segmenting words; and advancing spelling, writing, fluency, and reading comprehension across the genres. Reading progress requires monitoring and employing sensitivities to teach and communicate the appropriate skills and strategies to learners. Set up timetables that embrace IEP goals and literacy lesson objectives. Most important, allow students to own their reading strategies with structured task analysis and feedback. Encourage students to see how their perseverance has positive long-range effects by charting improvements (e.g., in fluency, comprehension, decoding) on graphed index cards and by listening to digital passages before and after set instructional timeframes. Keep digital portfolios and share these with students as visual and concrete reminders that monitor their efforts and increase awareness of literacy levels. Help students read words they may not have seen before by teaching strategies with proactive step-by-step visual and verbal directions. The following steps offer models that empower students to figure out a potentially tricky multisyllabic word, use context clues, and apply prior knowledge. A self-directed learner reads fluently with comprehension, knowing both pronunciation and word meanings both in isolation and with context.

To understand what you are reading . . .

1. Put your finger under the word to *ex-am-ine* and *chunk* it. See if there are syllables and word parts such as *un-der-stand* and *read-ing*. Find smaller words (e.g., *fan* in *fantastic*) or compound words (e.g., *bird's-eye*).
2. Look at illustrations that accompany the text and other words in the sentence or paragraph for clues that help you figure out what a word or sentence might mean. Ask yourself if you could substitute another word that means the same as the one you are reading. For example, *He admired his friend's decision* implies that *He respected his friend's actions and behaviors.*
3. Skip the word and read to the end of the sentence and paragraph to see if the context clues help you interpret the word's meaning. Give the words a chance to develop meaning. Sometimes, you need to read on before you understand what the author is saying.
4. If you still need help to read a "tricky word," then use an online or digital tool to pronounce the word, look it up in a dictionary, or ask a peer or adult.

Although using etymology, context clues, and a dictionary may be considered standard instruction for all students, learners with dyslexia require additional practice, varied engagements, multiple representations, and more time—along with vigilant progress monitoring—to achieve mastery. Ongoing feedback toward partial mastery acknowledges efforts toward achievement, which encourages more progress.

❂ Implement Multiple Representations

Providing representation options for learners with dyslexia means that instruction is not limited to printed text. Multiple representations reduce barriers and provide the same information through various modalities to ensure easier access and comprehension (CAST, 2011). When literacy instruction exists beyond two-dimensional worksheets, learners whose brains are wired differently are allowed multiple ways to decipher words and interpret text meaning. This includes offering learners diverse tools and resources (Cervetti, Damico, & Pearson, 2006).

The Orton-Gillingham approach (Academy of Orton-Gillingham Practitioners and Educators, 2012; Hwee & Houghton, 2011), which is based on neuroscience, propagates multisensory approaches for reading, spelling, and writing difficulties. Complex academic vocabulary in expository text in disciplines such as science and social studies sometimes fail to engage students (Marino, Gotch, Israel, Vasquez, Basham, & Becht, 2014). Increased auditory, visual, and kinesthetic-tactile approaches are employed to strengthen reading fluency and comprehension skills to better encode, decode, write, read, decipher, and understand written language. For example, students use their fingers to indicate or tap out the individual sounds of letters in words, which adds a tactile component. Other tactile approaches include forming and writing letters with clay, with shaving cream, on sandpaper, and in salt trays. Increased visuals allow some students to concretize letter sounds.

Another option is to present key words for vowel sounds; associate the short *e* sound with a picture of an elephant or the digraph *sh* with a picture of a finger by one's mouth to indicate quiet. When showing a video, activate the closed captioning so the auditory presentation is accompanied by the associated words. This assists primary- and secondary-level learners. In early grade levels, label classroom items and encourage families to do the same at home. If possible, provide advanced notes and partially filled-in organizers to lessen the writing requirements. As an example, allow students to concentrate on the content of a presentation instead of on the laborious task of taking notes. Notes available ahead of time also allows students to be more familiar with vocabulary that may not be in their prior knowledge. Sites such as Quizlet allow students to hear vocabulary read aloud and preview a word's meaning in isolation with digital and printed flashcards.

Use both low-tech and high-tech digital tools that honor and tap into students' stronger modalities and preferences to increase reading acumen. As an example, a student can use a sticky note to jot down a fact or question as he or she is reading text. A learner may prefer to use an app such as Post-it Plus to start conversations with peers and store information that is then looked at later. Handheld highlighters also offer digital ways to annotate and record text; the C-Pen uses Optimal Character Recognition (OCR) software. This higher-tech option captures text, decodes it, and then has the capability to transfer that information to a computer or smartphone. With this technology, unfamiliar and multisyllabic vocabulary is defined and spoken with reference tools and text-to-speech features activated. Each decision requires looking at each learner to determine the best instructional decision that may or may not include technology. The goal is to find a method that eases students' weaker areas and builds on each student's skills. Resources to consider include alternative reading formats, such as graphic novels, infographics, posters, e-books, apps, audiobooks, and online sites that target specific reading skills. Encourage struggling readers to pre-read while listening to audio or digital versions of the text to prepare them for class instruction. Use technology in class with instruction on how to use tools such as a digital thesaurus and spell check. Have students live-tweet answers to discussion questions on a Google Doc.

Handheld cue cards, checklists, and posted classroom wall charts are visual references that concretize what some learners with dyslexia view as abstract text. The letters, words, sentences, paragraphs, novels, and longer texts are not read with automaticity by most learners with dyslexia. Therefore, the provision of resources and accompanying strategies strengthen weaker reading skills and thereby increase self-efficacy. This includes dated progress reports and high-interest text across a variety of genres (from decoding words in poems to extracting information from online sites). If multiple students answer the same question, then the peer models offer additional insights for some learners. The goal is to guide students on a reading path that increases skills and self-efficacy. Provide the support with multiple representations, and then fade the scaffolding as students consistently and independently demonstrate literacy skills.

❯ Teach Decoding

Students who read slowly may require help with decoding and phonological awareness. Consider creating a classroom syllable wall chart (which continually grows as students add to it) to increase awareness of the various syllable types (see Figure 1.1). In addition, have students record the syllable charts in individual reading notebooks. Consider also dictating both simple and more complex sentences for students to hear, write, and self-correct. It's important that you're not the one who corrects errors. Offer opportunities for students to self-correct with a model provided. Provide instruction with both nonsense words and actual words to be certain that students are comfortable breaking the phonetic code—and not just memorizing words.

Figure 1.1 | Syllable Types

Closed	Open	Vowel-consonant-e	Vowel teams/ Diphthongs	Consonant-*le*	*r*-controlled
mat, wet, big, top, cup	go, me, hi, _label_, my, cozy	plate, mile, rope, time	air, boat, heat, stay	cand_le_, litt_le_, nob_le_	car, first, fur, burst

❯ Collaborate

Collaboration with staff, families, and students decreases the negative effects of dyslexia and highlights students' potential with moving their reading plans forward. Keep an eye on academic and social-emotional reading implications, with fidelity to the students, and share strategies with their families regarding the reading programs selected. Share reading progress and upcoming vocabulary and books on the school/class website or through regular (i.e., weekly or monthly) family newsletters. Communicate individual student progress in school-home journals and emails.

It's also important to collaborate with specialists, such as the speech-language pathologist for interventions that relate to phonics and phonemic awareness and occupational therapists for handwriting strategies and physical issues associated with dyslexia (e.g., slant board, alternative writing implements, specific handwriting programs, and ways to increase stamina).

In summation, it's critical that you can

- Identify characteristics of students with dyslexia and other reading disabilities and connect them to each learner's strengths.
- Use differentiated strategies to strengthen skills with sound-symbol association, fluency, spelling, comprehension, written expression, auditory and visual processing, and memory.
- Review multisensory ways to teach language with direct systematic instruction that honors learners' visual, auditory, and kinesthetic-tactile modalities.
- Use both low- and high-tech tools to help increase students' reading acumen.

References

Academy of Orton-Gillingham Practitioners and Educators. (2012). The Orton-Gillingham approach. Available: www.ortonacademy.org/approach.php

Alliance for Excellent Education. (2006). *Adolescent literacy (Fact Sheet)* Available: www.carnegie.org/publications/adolescent-literacy-fact-sheet

CAST. (2011). *Universal Design for Learning guidelines* (version 2.0). Wakefield, MA: Author.

Cervetti, G., Damico, J., & Pearson, P. (2006) Multiple literacies, new literacies, and teacher education. *Theory into Practice, 45*(4), 378–386.

Foss, B. (2013). *The dyslexia empowerment plan: A blueprint for renewing your child's confidence and love of reading.* New York: Ballantine.

Germanò, E., Gagliano, A., & Curatolo, P. (2010). Comorbidity of ADHD and dyslexia. *Developmental Neuropsychology, 35*(5), 475–493.

Guerin, A., & Murphy, B. (2015). Repeated reading as a method to improve reading fluency for struggling adolescent readers. *Journal of Adolescent & Adult Literacy, 58*(7), 551–560.

Hwee, N., & Houghton, S. (2011). The effectiveness of Orton-Gillingham-based instruction with Singaporean children with specific reading disability (dyslexia). *British Journal of Special Education, 38*(3), 143–149.

International Dyslexia Association, Professional Standards and Practices Committee. (2010). Knowledge and practice standards for teachers of reading. Available: https://eida.org/kps-for-teachers-of-reading

Kim, Y., & Wagner, R. (2015). Text oral reading fluency as a construct in reading development: An investigation of its mediating role for children from grades 1-4. *Scientific Studies of Reading, 19*(3), 224–242.

Lyon, G., Shaywitz, S., & Shaywitz, B. (2003). Defining dyslexia, comorbidity, teachers' knowledge of language and reading. *Annals of Dyslexia, 53*, 1–14.

Marino, M., Gotch, C., Israel, M., Vasquez, E., Basham, J., & Becht, K. (2014). UDL in the middle school science classroom: Can video games and alternative text heighten engagement and learning for students with learning disabilities? *Learning Disability Quarterly, 37*(2), 87–99.

Moats, L. C., & Dakin, K. E. (2008). *Basic facts about dyslexia and other reading problems.* Baltimore: International Dyslexia Association.

National Center for Learning Disabilities. (2015). 13 organizations urge U.S. Department of Education to tell states: It's okay to use terms like "dyslexia" in IEP. Contributors of www.ncld.org

Siegel, L. S. (2006). Perspectives on dyslexia. *Paediatrics & Child Health, 11*(9), 581–587.

Snowling, M. (2012). Changing concepts of dyslexia: nature, treatment and comorbidity. *Journal of Child Psychology & Psychiatry, 53*(9), e1–e3.

State of New Jersey Department of Education. (n.d.). Dyslexia. Available: www.state.nj.us/education/specialed/dyslexia/pd.shtml

Torgesen, J., Foorman, B., & Wagner, R. (2007). FCRR Technical Report #8. Dyslexia: A brief for educators, parents, and legislators in Florida. Available: http://files.eric.ed.gov/fulltext/ED542605.pdf

Wagner, R., & Torgesen, J. (1987). The nature of phonological processing and its causal role in the acquisition of reading skills. *Psychological Bulletin, 101*, 192–212.

Professional Resources

Barden, O. (2009). From "acting reading" to reading for acting: A case study of the transformational power of reading. *Journal of Adolescent & Adult Literacy, 53*(4), 293–302.

Berninger, V., Lee, Y., Abbott, R., & Breznitz, Z. (2013). Teaching children with dyslexia to spell in a reading-writers' workshop. *Annals of Dyslexia, 63*(1), 1–24.

Bonifacci, P., Montuschi, M., Lami, L., & Snowling, M. (2014). Parents of children with dyslexia: Cognitive, emotional, and behavioural profile. *Dyslexia, 20*(2), 175–190.

Brackley, L. (2015). A response to Elliott. *Psychology of Education Review, 39*(1) 28–31.

Dyslexia Buddy Network: www.dyslexiabuddynetwork.com

Flocabulary Songs and Videos: www.flocabulary.com

Hachmann, W. M., Bogaerts, L., Szmalec, A., Woumans, E., Duyck, W., & Job, R. (2014). Short-term memory for order but not for item information is impaired in developmental dyslexia. *Annals of Dyslexia, 64*(2), 121–136.

Hulme, C., & Snowling, M. J. (2013). Learning to read: What we know and what we need to understand better. *Child Development Perspectives, 7*(1), 1–5.

Hurley, K. S. (2013). *What is dyslexia?* TED Talk. Available: http://ed.ted.com/lessons/what-is-dyslexia-kelli-sandman-hurley

International Dyslexia Association (IDA): http://eida.org

IDA-Testing and Evaluation: https://dyslexiaida.org/testing-and-evaluation/

National Council of Teachers of English. *Read write think*: www.readwritethink.org

Newsela: https://newsela.com

Nielsen, C. (2011). The most important thing: Students with reading and writing difficulties talk about their experiences of teachers' treatment and guidance. *Scandinavian Journal of Educational Research, 55*(5), 551–565.

Paul, A. (2012, February 5). The upside of dyslexia. *New York Times*. Available: www.nytimes.com/2012/02/05/opinion/sunday/the-upside-of-dyslexia.html?_r=1

Pongrey, M. Dyslexia and high school. *LD Online*. Available: www.ldonline.org/article/25150

Quick Phonics Screener: www.readnaturally.com/products/qps.htm

Quizlet—Vocabulary, Flashcards, Games: https://quizlet.com

Rakhlin, N., Cardoso-Martins, C., Kornilov, S., & Grigorenko, E. (2013). Spelling well despite developmental language disorder: What makes it possible? *Annals of Dyslexia, 63*(3–4), 253–273.

Readworks: www.readworks.org

Smithsonian Tween Tribune: http://tweentribune.com

Starfall: www.starfall.com

Stetter, M. E., & Hughes, M. T. (2010). Computer-assisted instruction to enhance the reading comprehension of struggling readers: A review of the literature. *Journal of Special Education Technology, 25*(4), 1–16.

Storyonline: www.storylineonline.net

Tar Heel Reader: http://tarheelreader.org

University of Michigan. (2016). Tests for dyslexia and learning disabilities. The regents of the University of Michigan. Available: http://dyslexiahelp.umich.edu/dyslexics/learn-about-dyslexia/dyslexia-testing/tests

Washburn, E. K., Joshi, R. M., & Binks-Cantrell, E. S. (2011). Teacher knowledge of basic language concepts and dyslexia. *Dyslexia, 17*(2), 165–183.

Yale Center for Dyslexia and Creativity: http://dyslexia.yale.edu

2

Students with Attention Deficit Hyperactivity Disorder (ADHD)

The Possible Whys

The exact cause of attention deficit hyperactivity disorder (ADHD) is unknown, but research shows that it is a result of an imbalance of neurotransmitters—chemical messengers in the brain that help brain cells communicate with one another (Gromisch, 2016). ADHD is recognized as a legitimate diagnosis by major medical, psychological, and educational organizations, including the National Institutes of Health and the U.S. Department of Education. The American Psychiatric Association (APA) recognizes ADHD as a medical disorder in its *Diagnostic and Statistical Manual of Mental Disorders* (DSM-5, 2013).

Attention deficit hyperactivity disorder is not imagined, nor is it a result of a student's lack of effort; it is biologically based. Documented areas of the brain affected include the prefrontal and frontal lobes, basal ganglia, and cerebellum. Genetic and molecular studies suggest hereditary factors (Rosen, 2014), but since it runs in families, some theories also point to environmental factors, such as foods, toxins, and psychosocial factors (Banarjee, Middleton, & Faraone, 2007). The cause, however, is rooted in brain chemistry—not a lack of discipline. Specifically, it's rooted in levels of the neurotransmitter dopamine (which helps regulate movement and emotional responses) and the hormone norepinephrine (which is involved in the body's reaction to stress) (Hunt, 2006). Additional theories about possible causes of ADHD include toxic exposure to lead and pesticides (Banarjee et al., 2007), alcohol consumption and smoking during pregnancy (Grominus, Ridout, Sandberg, & Santosh, 2009), and poor nutrition or diet (Harvard Medical School, 2009). Research studies also document ADHD with twins, along with comorbidity (Taylor, Charman, & Ronald, 2015): if one twin has ADHD, then it's highly likely the other does as well (Freitag & Retz, 2010). It is important to note that even though each twin may have ADHD, their symptoms may not be identical.

Characteristics and Strengths

As noted, students with ADHD have differences in brain activity and structure that help control behavior and attention. Thus, they often have challenges with rule-governed behavior, attention, time management, persistence on task, and organizational skills. However, it is important to keep in mind that learners with ADHD also have strengths, likes, and interests that need to be acknowledged. As with all differences, no two students with ADHD display identical characteristics. Each child is unique.

In 2011–2013, 9.5 percent of children age 4–17 were diagnosed with ADHD. For those age 4–5, the prevalence was 2.7 percent, 9.5 percent for those age 6–11, and 11.8 percent for those age 12–17 (CDC, 2015). ADHD is evidenced by both sexes; females are sometimes more inattentive than hyperactive and are, at times, underdiagnosed. Boys outnumber girls at least 2 to 1. According to DSM-5, symptoms are typically documented prior to age 12 (APA, 2013). In addition, a diagnosis of ADHD may have a child present with social differences that are associated with autism spectrum disorder (ASD; see Chapter 8). However, the extent of how much these symptoms overlap needs more documentation (Grzadzinski, Dick, Lord, & Bishop, 2016).

Learners diagnosed with ADHD may have combined symptoms of both inattention and hyperactivity-impulsivity, which need to be present for six consecutive months, or they may display predominantly inattentive or predominantly hyperactive-impulsive behavior. The following lists outline the characteristics of the three types of ADHD:

ADHD, Predominantly Inattentive Type
- Inattention: lack of attention to details, difficulty sustaining attention, challenges with organization, distractibility

ADHD, Predominantly Hyperactive-Impulsive Type
- Hyperactivity: fidgeting, leaving one's seat, talking excessively
- Impulsivity: having difficulty waiting one's turn, interrupting others

ADHD, Combined Type
- Inattention, hyperactivity, and/or impulsivity

In general, students display inattention with times of daydreaming, disorganization, memory difficulties, and a minimization of or disregard for what appear to be obvious details. If students are predominantly hyperactive-impulsive, then they are more reactionary and fidgety, and they may be in constant motion.

Psychological and behavioral characteristics include deficits in executive function (see Chapter 5) that affect impulse control, working memory, and organizational skills. Three areas that affect academic performance and student success in school that require close attention when working with a student with ADHD include the child's organization skills, social development, and behavior management/self-regulation (Johnson & Reid, 2011). Social, emotional, and behavioral differences (see Chapter 3) affect the ability to control inhibitions; develop peer relationships; and follow school and classroom rules, routines, and structures. In addition, coexisting conditions may overlap with learning disabilities (see Chapter 4) and emotional and behavioral disorders. When students are older, substance abuse is sometimes evidenced.

School staff should be prepared to address the following possible ADHD behaviors (Karten, 2015):

- Daydreaming
- Less care and attention to schoolwork (e.g., poor handwriting, crumpled homework)
- Forgetfulness
- Disorganization (e.g., lost things)
- Distractibility
- Concentration and listening challenges (e.g., attending to the teacher while trying to take notes)
- Attention difficulties when initiating actions that require foresight
- Impulsivity (e.g., blurting out answers)
- Challenges when shifting gears or transitioning to other tasks
- Difficulties following multistep directions
- Frequent motion
- Fidgeting with hands or feet (e.g., rocking in chair, tapping feet)
- Missing social cues, getting into fights
- Difficulty waiting one's turn (e.g., interrupting others)
- Accidents due to hyperactivity

Ed Hallowell, a psychiatrist and ADHD specialist, explains that having ADHD is like having a Ferrari engine for a brain but with bicycle brakes (in News Medical Life Sciences & Medicine, 2014). More than 70 percent of the individuals who have ADHD in childhood continue to have it in adolescence. Up to 50 percent will continue to have it in adulthood. Although it has been estimated that 6 percent of the adult population has ADHD, the majority of those adults remain undiagnosed, and only one in four of them seek treatment (ADDitude, 2005).

Classroom Implications

ADHD is not recognized as a separate category of special education under the Individuals with Disabilities Education Act (IDEA). However, a student with ADHD who receives special education services is most often offered services under IDEA's category of Other Health Impaired (OHI) and/or receives accommodations under Section 504.

Classroom structure and teacher direction are particularly essential for learners with ADHD as they assist with students' organization capabilities and contingency-based self-management. It is important to hone social development with behavior management plans. Contingency management allows a learner to receive something desirable, based or contingent on performing what the student may consider a less desirable task or behavior. It is likened to the Premack principle or Grandma's law (Center for Effective Collaboration and Practice, 1998), which is commonly described with a statement such as "If you complete the entire math assignment with 80 percent accuracy, then you can have free time on the computer." A less desirable behavior or activity, such as staying in one's seat, is the hinge that determines whether the student is "rewarded" with a more desirable activity, such as helping the teacher pass out worksheets.

Students with ADHD often have challenges when memory demands increase beyond rote memorization and require working memory (Vakil, Blachstein, Wertman-Elad, & Greenstein, 2011). Some students are excellent memorizers, but when they are asked the same questions several days later, their responses do not always match their earlier ones. Quite often, students who do well on tests do not always have a true grasp of the learning material. The goal is to solidify and internalize the learning by getting to the core of each student to better understand his or her needs, interests, and overall internal triggers. Offering students with ADHD additional reference tools, wait time to process, or extra time to complete an assignment or test may be one way to help them tap their working memories.

School staff need to be aware of each learner's behavioral and medical treatment plans (if appropriate). For example, if a student with ADHD is on medication, then he or she may have side effects such as headaches, low appetite, and erratic sleep patterns that manifest as inconsistent school performance. In addition, medical interventions may not be limited to one drug, whether it is a stimulant or nonstimulant.

Many treatments today are multimodal, with increased awareness and strategies offered for students, staff, and families.

Behavior therapy is essential to boost self-efficacy. For learners with ADHD, behavior therapy includes reinforcers that assist with hyperactivity, impulse control, and attention. This involves intrinsic and extrinsic motivators—from smiles to certificates, stars, and additional free time. Both abstract and concrete items are specific to each learner. This includes verbal praise, point systems, or perhaps a visit to the prize box for an elementary school student or extra time in art or chorus for a middle school or high school student. Sometimes, students act a certain way to receive attention, whether it is positive or negative. Awareness of specific antecedents for behavior or lack of attention and/or impulsivity or the hyperactivity that is evidenced drives the classroom approaches. Collaborators include guidance counselors, school psychologists, behavior interventionists, administration, and general or special education staff—along with families and students.

Finally, school staff and teachers must remember that medications may reduce unwanted behaviors, but they do not replace the student's self-management plans or the family's and teacher's responsibilities.

Inclusion Strategies

❯ Offer the Appropriate Instructional Support

Teachers can readily provide effective and appropriate instructional supports to students with ADHD; "it does not have to be a costly or time-consuming process" (Stormont, 2008, p. 308). Since no two students with ADHD display identical characteristics, adaptations should be student-specific. Always keep in mind that students with ADHD are not defined by the inappropriate behavior they may display.

❯ Organize and Structure

Model and offer help with organization, such as showing how to record homework, checking intermittently on long-term assignments, monitoring the accuracy of student notes, providing a weekly calendar of class and school events, and offering assistance to reduce clutter.

Research indicates that students learn best when material is repeated and practiced to lock it into their long-term memory (Willingham, 2004). Students with ADHD, especially, require repeated exposure to concepts to avoid memorizing unrelated facts and to attain strong understanding. Post routines and schedules in the same location. Older elementary and secondary students can be reminded about assignment with websites, online calendars, and appropriate apps such as Remind.

❯ Monitor to Advance Attention

It is vital that a student with ADHD, his or her family, and staff monitor the student's behavior in response to interventions to reinforce positive attention, behavior, and academic strides. Such ongoing monitoring includes observations and both formal and informal assessments.

Use signals (e.g., a raised hand, a wink) to increase a student's attention during lectures, and follow through with age-appropriate "rewards" (e.g., additional PE time, a sticker, or simply a smile). Implement curriculum-based management tools, such as rating scales, direct observations, and behavioral recording systems. As stated earlier, one effective behavior management system is contingency-based self-management. This approach "usually involves having [students] keep track of behavior and then receive consequences, usually in the form of rewards, based on their behavior" (Hallahan, Kauffman, & Pullen, 2015, p. 165). Contingency management shapes and rewards more desirable actions. If a student with ADHD pays attention, follows the rules, and works within the class structure, then he or she receives a favorable result—for example, more time working on the computer or playing with LEGO bricks. Staff members provide increased observation to ensure accurate self-reflection, along with additional feedback. If the class is cotaught or has an instructional assistant or paraprofessional present, then the ratio is lowered to ensure that student behavior receives additional scrutiny to reinforce appropriate actions and extinguish less desirable ones. Quick response increases learner attention, the accurate completion of academic tasks, and productive social interactions during whole-class and small-group instruction.

Another effective way to monitor a student with ADHD is informal momentary time sampling procedures, which involve looking at a behavior during a set time period to note the frequency of occurrence (see Figure 2.1). For example, during a 50-minute class period, the frequency of a behavior is noted for ten consecutive five-minute intervals with tally marks or a Y (yes) or N (no). Behaviors include following directions, maintaining eye contact, speaking appropriately, and interacting respectfully with peers and/or adults. These behaviors are stated in positive terms: "I make eye contact with the teacher" versus "I don't ignore the teacher." Depending on the student's age and grade level, actions are monitored and noted by the student or a staff member (e.g., a coteacher or an instructional assistant).

More formal monitoring examples include Vanderbilt and Conners's ADHD Parent and Teacher Rating Scales (ADHD & You Screening Tools, 2016). Use the collected data to guide instructional and behavioral supports and decisions.

Figure 2.1 | Momentary Behavioral Time Sampling

Date: 12/08/2017 Every 10 minutes	Time Period										Total times that the behavior happened (Y)
Eye Contact	1	2	3	4	5	6	7	8	9	10	
Yes (Y) or No (N)	Y	N	Y	N	Y	N	Y	Y	N	Y	6

◗ Communicate, Collaborate, Connect

Communicate your expectations clearly, with simple verbal and written reminders, as well as with rubrics for essays and interim checks for long-term assignments. Provide examples and nonexamples. When possible, connect to students' interests and strengths during instruction and in assessments. General education teachers who "demonstrate patience, knowledge of intervention techniques, an ability to collaborate with an interdisciplinary team, and a positive attitude towards children with special needs can have a positive impact on student success" (Sherman, Rasmussen, & Baydala, 2008, p. 347).

Collaboration with students involves sharing learning objectives, revisiting them, and dissecting which parts of the objectives require additional follow-through. Collaborate with families in reference to both behavioral and academic domains. This home-school connection sends a strong message that everyone is on the same team. Sharing effective strategies that are continued in home environments offers the consistency, repetition, and reinforcement that help students with ADHD thrive. Collaboration also includes all school staff in the ADHD loop: the general and special education teachers, school nurse, subject-matter teachers, guidance counselor, assistant principal, lunchroom aides, school bus drivers, and so forth.

◗ Honor Learning Styles and Kinesthetic Approaches

All students have different learning styles. Even though students with ADHD respond well to structure, the delivery of the concepts and strategies needs to go beyond lectures to honor their individuality and to promote increased attention, retention, and applications. Some learners prefer dim lighting, shorter time periods with breaks, kinesthetic and tactile resources, or verbal encouragement (Brand, Dunn, & Greb, 2002). Active and experiential (not passive) learning within fun, engaging classroom environments enhances memory and retrieval (Kuczala, & McCall, 2011). Think of novel ways to deliver instruction that offer students physical exercise to help focus their attention, and then channel the impulsivity and hyperactivity that students with ADHD might display. The following examples across the curriculum include active engagement:

- *Social Studies:* Students receive sticky notes with labeled continents and move to spots around the room to demonstrate locations that simulate a world map.
- *Writing:* Students are provided with quiet "think spots" in the classroom to use reference materials and compose and revise their written work.
- *Math:* Learners identify spatial figures around the school, move to imitate translations and reflections, and measure the height of classroom objects.
- *Science:* A high school science teacher places his students in human electron configurations to actively teach the Pauli exclusion principle (Kuczala & McCall, 2011).
- *Reading, Art, and Music:* Students create storyboards for the events in a play or a mind map from the points of view of a novel's protagonist and antagonist, create a song about a story's events, or use the comic creator from the National Council of Teachers of English (www.readwritethink.org) to create dialogue depicting a scene from a book.

The point is to offer students productive yet structured learning options—a choice of writing assignments based on interests or the option to create a YouTube video, poem, dance, or song about a topic. Encourage independence, and most certainly infuse your teaching with humor to lighten any anxiety on the part of your students with ADHD—or your own!

❍ Partner to Increase Awareness

Increase awareness of how personal improvement plans improve school performance, social interactions, and behavioral decisions with peers and adults in school, home, and community settings. For example, offer conflict resolution training to staff and students with ADHD to improve communication skills and reduce potential tensions in the classroom (Barkley, 2014; Hamilton & Astramovich, 2016). Help students understand how they learn and how to use different metacognitive strategies to plan, monitor, and reflect on their learning, as well as being cognizant of their motivations and emotions (González, 2013).

As mentioned at the start of this chapter, students with ADHD may benefit from a behavior management system that focuses on self-monitoring (Martinussen, Tannock, & Chaban, 2010). This approach includes developing increased reflection and self-awareness and targeting short- and long-term goals. A student goal can be stated as simply as that shown in Figure 2.2, citing the targeted goal and ideal date for achieving it.

Figure 2.2 | Personal Goal Statement

My Personal Goal Statement

I plan to _____ by _____.

(Date)

Heightened awareness for students with ADHD also means that students try to

- Turn verbal plans into concrete viable actions.
- Avoid viewing setbacks or criticism as excuses to stop trying.
- Spin negative learning experiences into positive ones.
- Reflect on how their behavior affects others.
- Communicate their needs and concerns.
- Invite peers, family, and educators to be partners—not adversaries.

To sum up this chapter, it's important to be an advocate of your students with ADHD by

- Varying instruction and engagement.
- Introducing lessons in novel, attention-getting ways for increased retention.
- Teaching students how to channel their impulses in acceptable ways (e.g., squeezing a ball).
- Having students jot down ideas on sticky notes before interrupting lesson flow.
- Encouraging self-regulation.
- Offering realistic, timely, and specific feedback.
- Coordinating strategies with staff, families, students, and student peers.
- Exploring ways to advance attention—not chastise noncompliance.
- Being patient but firm and consistent in your expectations and objectives.
- Definitely keeping your cool.

References

ADDitude. (2005). 7 myths about ADHD debunked. Available: www.additudemag.com/adhd/article/873.html

ADHD & You: Screening and diagnostic tools for use with children/teenagers. (2016). Lexington, MA: Shire. Available: www.adhdandyou.com/hcp/children-adhd-screening.aspx

American Psychiatric Association. (2013). *Diagnostic and statistical manual of mental disorders* (5th ed.). Washington, DC: Author.

Banarjee, T., Middleton, F., & Faraone, S. (2007). Environmental risk factors for students with attention-deficit hyperactivity disorder. *Acta Paediatrica, 96*(9) 1269–1274.

Barkley, R. A. (2014). *Attention-deficit hyperactivity disorder: A handbook for diagnosis and treatment.* New York: Guilford.

Brand, S., Dunn, R., & Greb, F. (2002). Learning styles of students with attention deficit hyperactivity disorder: Who are they and how can we teach them? *Clearing House, 75*(5), 268–273.

Center for Effective Collaboration and Practice. (1998). Contingency management information for families. Available: http://cecp.air.org/familybriefs/docs/CONTINGENCY.pdf

Centers for Disease Control and Prevention (CDC). (2015). Attention-deficit hyperactivity disorders. Available: www.cdc.gov/nchs/data/databriefs/db201.htm

Freitag, C. M., & Retz, W. (2010). Family and twin studies in attention-deficit hyperactivity disorder. In W. Retz & R.G. Klein (Eds.), *Attention-Deficit Hyperactivity Disorder (ADHD) in adults: Key issues in mental health.* (Vol. 176, pp. 38–57). Available: http://content.karger.com/produktedb/katalogteile/isbn3_8055/_92/_37/kimh176_02.pdf

González, M. (2013). Learning goals and strategies in self-regulated learning. *US-China Educational Review A, 3*(1), 46–50.

Grominus, R., Ridout, D., Sandberg, S., & Santosh, P. (2009). Maternal alcohol consumption. *London Journal of Primary Care, 2*(1) 28–35.

Grzadzinski, R., Dick, C., Lord, C., & Bishop, S. (2016). Parent reported and clinician-observed autism spectrum disorder (ASD) symptoms in children with attention deficit/hyperactivity disorder (ADHD): Implications for practice under DSM-5. *Molecular Autism, 7*, 1–12.

Hallahan, D., Kauffman, J., & Pullen, P. (2015). *Exceptional learners: An introduction to special education.* Upper Saddle River, NJ: Pearson.

Hamilton, N., & Astramovich, R. (2016). Teaching strategies for students with ADHD: Findings from the field. *Education, 136*(4), 451–460.

Harvard Medical School (2009). Diet and attention hyperactivity disorder, Harvard Health Publications, Available: www.health.harvard.edu/newsletter_article/Diet-and-attention-deficit-hyperactivity-disorder

Hunt, R. (2006). Functional roles of norepinephrine and dopamine in ADHD. *Medscape Psychiatry* Available: www.medscape.org/viewarticle/523887

Johnson, J., & Reid, R. (2011). Overcoming executive function deficits with students with ADHD. *Theory into Practice, 50*(1) 61–67.

Karten, T. (2015). *Inclusion strategies that work* (3rd ed.). Thousand Oaks, CA: Corwin.

Kuczala, M., & McCall, J. (2011, April). Get your students moving! *New Jersey Education Association Review*. Available: www.njea.org/news-and-publications/njea-review/april-2011/get-your-students-moving

Martinussen, R., Tannock, R., & Chaban, P. (2010). Teachers' reported use of instructional and behavior management practice for students with behavior problems: Relationship to role and level of training in ADHD. *Child Youth Care Forum, 40,* 193–210.

News Medical Life Sciences & Medicine. (2014). Neuropsychologist sees increase in ADHD diagnoses. Available: www.news-medical.net/news/20140902/Neuropsychologist-sees-increase-in-ADHD-diagnoses.aspx

Sherman, J., Rasmussen, C., & Baydala, L. (2008). The impact of teacher factors on achievement and behavioral outcomes of children with attention deficit/hyperactivity disorder (ADHD): A review of the literature. *Educational Research, 50*(4), 347–360.

Stormont, M. (2008). Increase academic success for children with ADHD using sticky notes and highlighters. *Intervention in School and Clinic, 43*(5), 305–308.

Taylor, M., Charman, T., & Ronald, A. (2015). Where are the strongest associations between autistic traits and traits of ADHD? Evidence from a community-based twin study. *European Child & Adolescent Psychiatry, 24*(9), 1129–1138.

Vakil, E., Blachstein, H., Wertman-Elad, R., & Greenstein, Y. (2011). Verbal learning and memory as measured by the Rey-auditory verbal learning test: ADHD with and without learning disabilities. *Child Neuropsychology, 18*(5), 449–466.

Willingham, D. T. (2004). Understanding ADHD. Available: www.aft.org/periodical/american-educator/winter-2004-2005/ask-cognitive-scientist

Professional Resources

ADDitude: Strategies and Support for ADHD & LD. Available: www.additudemag.com

ADHD Popplet: http://popplet.com/app/#/1959672

Attention Deficit Disorder Association: www.add.org

Centers for Disease Control and Prevention. (2015). Available: www.cdc.gov/ncbddd/adhd/data.html

CHAAD: The National Resource on ADHD (2016). Available: www.help4adhd.org/Understanding-ADHD/About-ADHD.aspx

Children and Adults with Attention-Deficit/Hyperactivity Disorder (CHADD): www.chadd.org

Cohen, S., & Schwarz, A. (2013, March 31). A.D.H.D seen in 11% of U.S. children as diagnoses rise. *New York Times*. Available: www.nytimes.com/2013/04/01/health/more-diagnoses-of-hyperactivity-causing-concern

DuPaul, G. J., Weyandt, L. L., & Janusis, G. M. (2011). ADHD in the classroom: Effective intervention strategies. *Theory into Practice, 50*(1), 35–42.

Gehret, J. (2009). *Eagle eyes: A child's guide to paying attention.* Fairport, NY: Verbal Images Press.

Gromisch, E. (17 Jul 2016) Neurotransmitters involved in ADHD, *PsychCentral.* Available: http://psychcentral.com/lib/neurotransmitters-involved-in-adhd

Hamilton, N., & Astramovich, R. (2016). Teaching strategies for students with ADHD: Findings from the field. *Education, 136*(4), 451–460.

Hoopmann, K. (2008). *All dogs have ADHD.* Philadelphia: Kingsley.

Langberg, J., Epstein, J., & Graham, A. (2008). Organizational-skills interventions in the treatment of ADHD. *Expert Review Neurotherapeutics, 10,* 1549–1561.

Martinussen, R. (2015). The overlap of ADHD, reading disorders, and language impairment. *Perspectives on Language and Literacy, 41*(1), 9–14.

National Institute of Mental Health RSS. (2015, September 22). Attention deficit hyperactivity disorder. Available: www.nimh.nih.gov/health/topics/attention-deficit-hyperactivity-disorder-adhd/index.shtml

Remind: www.remind.com

Rosen, P. (2014). At a glance: Learning and attention issues and the brain. *Understood.* Available: www.understood.org/en/learning-attention-issues/getting-started/what-you-need-to-know/learning-and-attention-issues-and-the-brain

Stern, J., & Quinn, P. O. (2009). *Putting on the brakes: Activity book for kids with ADHD or ADD.* Washington, DC: Magination Press.

Sherman, J., Rasmussen, C., & Baydala, L. (2006). Thinking positively: How some characteristics of ADHD can be adaptive and accepted in the classroom. *Childhood Education, 82*(4), 196–200.

Shillingford-Butler, M., & Theodore, L. (2013). Students diagnosed with attention deficit hyperactivity disorder: Collaborative strategies for school counselors. *Professional School Counseling, 16*(4), 235–244.

Stamp, L., Banerjee, M., & Brown, F. C. (2014). Self-advocacy and perceptions of college readiness among students with ADHD. *Journal of Postsecondary Education and Disability, 27*(2), 139–160.

Zambo, D. (2008). Looking at ADHD through multiple lenses: Identifying girls with the inattentive type. *Intervention in School and Clinic, 44*(1), 34–40.

3
Students with Social, Emotional, and Behavioral Differences

The Possible Whys

Many factors can lead to emotional, behavioral, and social differences, including biological, environmental, cultural, and family factors. These include but are not limited to heredity, chemical imbalances in the brain, anxiety, stress, diet, substance and parental abuse, and inappropriate school programs (Center for Parent Information and Resources, 2015). No one can pinpoint an exact cause of emotional disturbance, but as the Individuals with Disabilities Act (IDEA) states, the condition occurs over a long period of time and is not explained by intellectual, sensory, or health factors.

Characteristics and Strengths

Examples of social, emotional, and behavioral characteristics are not always clear cut because they often overlap. Emotional disturbance is a classification from IDEA, but this chapter refers to emotional *differences* to emphasize a positive perspective on a disability that is often viewed through a negative lens and consequently misunderstood in schools and communities. Emotional difference is a broad category that includes internalizing and externalizing behaviors, with an overlapping of characteristics sometimes evidenced. Internalizing behaviors include depression, eating disorders, compulsive behavior, rituals, excessive anxiety, and mood swings. Externalizing behaviors are negative actions directed outward toward others, such as destruction of property, refusal to follow rules, verbal bullying, defiance, theft, physical aggression, and harmful behaviors exhibited with peer and adult interactions. A type of externalizing behavior includes a conduct disorder that is disruptive and often violent with characteristics such as aggression, deceit, bullying, and defiance (Child & Adolescent Psychiatry, 2013). Internalizing and externalizing behaviors may also accompany diagnoses such as obsessive-compulsive disorder (OCD), oppositional defiant disorder (ODD), bipolar disorder, and selective mutism.

Variation, confusion, and controversy over names and terms are common. Overall, an emotional disturbance is not a temporary reaction to stress, such as a death in the family or a divorce. Classification is further complicated because students are often not correctly identified due to the stigma associated with mental illness, an error in teacher judgment, or a lack of triggers at school that prompt the behavior. IDEA's description of emotional disturbance includes an inability to build or maintain satisfactory interpersonal relationships with peers and teachers, along with a general pervasive mood of unhappiness or depression, inappropriate types of behavior under normal circumstances over a long period of time, and a tendency to develop physical symptoms (e.g., a stomachache) or fears in reference to personal and/or school challenges. Moreover, the differences exhibited adversely affect a student's performance.

Confusion and controversy are also common because of the differences among emotional, social, and behavioral characteristics and other disabilities. As examples, a student with autism may display less ease with peer interactions and social reciprocity, a student with traumatic brain injury can display acting-out behavior due to frustration, a student with ADHD may express less concern over behavioral infractions, and a student with dyslexia may display anxiety. Also, note a student's functional performance, which references how he or she performs nonacademic tasks. Within a student's IEP, academic and functional levels are outlined; this includes both learning goals and how a student handles daily living routines. Functional skills involve levels of independence and a display of autonomy, ranging from dressing oneself to displaying appropriate hygiene, reading street signs, knowing the value of money, and demonstrating appropriate classroom, school, and community navigations and interactions.

As with other differences, it's important to see beyond the behavior exhibited and the associated label to the core of each student and be aware of the comorbidity and range of characteristics that exist. Even though a student's behavior is deemed inappropriate at times, staff need to note a learner's positive characteristics. A learner should never be defined by his or her emotional, behavioral, or social difference. Like flowers, learners are diverse. Realistic praise and feedback promotes increased self-esteem and often replaces negative emotions, interactions, and behaviors. Strengths exist within each learner. Whether a student is better at drawing, writing, car mechanics, cosmetology, or astronomy, capitalize and recognize each learner's individual strengths.

Classroom Implications

Each student has a story that staff need to see, hear, and respond to with the appropriate interventions that match that student's behavioral, social, and emotional levels. Sometimes students tell a quiet story with soft signs that cannot be ignored. If a student starts to come to school looking unkempt, wearing dark clothes exclusively, or communicating depressing thoughts in writing or through actions, it's critical to respond to these signs. Sometimes a student's story varies within a given week, day, or hour. Observe your students. Many emotions are of titanic proportions but exist below the surface. Remember to notice the quieter students who are silently screaming for responsive interventions. If a student acts out with externalizing behavior, remember to clearly communicate that you dislike his or her *behavior,* not the student. It is difficult but vital to separate the two. Alert peers to do the same. Proactively state and reinforce nonnegotiable class rules, and honor the consequences for the infractions. Be consistent, fair, and firm—always protecting the safety of all students.

Be certain to determine whether the behavior is a manifestation of his or her disability. Manifestation determination is legislatively driven if a student—who violates a code of conduct—is to be removed from his or her school placement for more than 10 consecutive days. It is then determined if the behavior is related to the disability or if the behavior is the result of the local education agency's (LEA) failure to implement the IEP (Brownley, 2014; U.S. Department of Education, Sec. 300.530). If it is determined that the behavior is a manifestation of a student's disability, then a functional behavioral assessment (FBA) is conducted to determine why the behavior occurred. This then results in the modification of a behavioral intervention plan (BIP)—if one exists—or the development of a BIP if there is not already one in place. The BIP is listed in a student's individualized education program (IEP)—the document required by IDEA for students with disabilities. Remember that a student who chooses not to do work is likely doing so for a variety of reasons. Sometimes he or she is frustrated by the level of difficulty, is uninterested in the assignment, or is seeking attention. A student would often rather act out than admit he or she does not know an answer. Staff might believe the student is having a discipline issue when in fact the student is simply frustrated. At other times, lessons may not be challenging enough for some students, and they, too, may display inappropriate behaviors.

When the FBA is conducted, the reason for certain persistent, unwarranted behaviors is determined by the IEP team. The FBA results in the selection and implementation of the appropriate interventions. An FBA usually leads to a more formal BIP. BIPs include positive reinforcement and individualized behavior plans. Even if there is no formal BIP, a teacher can prepare an informal one for a given student with contingencies built in to increase positive behavior. Informal BIPs include monitoring and reinforcements that are designed to replace inappropriate behaviors with more positive ones. Always observe, record, share, and reinforce behavior and note the antecedents. If it is a cotaught class or an instructional assistant or paraprofessional is present, collaborate to share responsibilities for monitoring and promoting positive learner behaviors with all staff having a role to observe, record data, scaffold, and reinforce.

Inclusion Strategies

⊘ Understand Your Students, and Let Your Students Understand Themselves

Invite students to own and reflect on their behaviors with emotional regulation, social interactions, and ways to increase their self-perceptions. Staff members need to realize that just as a student with dyslexia cannot magically read on request, a student with social, behavioral, and emotional differences requires time and scaffolding to own and apply the appropriate behaviors. Learn more about your students by inviting them to share their daily concerns and by talking to them, their families, and former teachers. Find out their favorite activities with observations, interest inventories, and ongoing conversations. Then infuse some of these activities into your instruction and assignments to promote positive emotional, social, and behavioral traits. Consider the following strategies:

- Discuss compare-contrast situations with students that clearly outline the similarities and differences from one day to the next with different procedures followed, behaviors exhibited, and consequences experienced to string together emotional-social-behavioral threads. As an example, "Yesterday you were out of your seat three times in ten minutes and missed writing important class notes, but today because you were focused with eye contact, stayed in your seat, and paid attention, your notes are perfect."
- Read books in class or ask your students to read books at home that examine emotions in nonthreatening ways (see Appendix D)—for example, *When My Worries Get Too Big: A Relaxation Book for Children Who Live with Anxiety* by Kari Dunn Buron; *Cool, Calm, and Confident: A Workbook to Help Kids Learn Assertiveness Skills* by Lisa M. Schab; and *The Mindful Teen: Powerful Skills to Help You Handle Stress, One Moment at a Time* by Dzung X. Vo.
- Try role-playing to explore behaviors.
- Offer low- and high-tech tools to increase learner awareness of eye contact, tone of voice and inflection, positive behaviors, body language, and social

reciprocity during whole-class and small-group instruction (e.g., www.classdojo.com is an online communication profile that uses avatars to reinforce positive behavior ; www.do2learn.com is a site with resources and activities to increase social skills and behavioral regulation, video modeling, student-teacher conferencing, and behavioral tally sheets).

- Invite students to acknowledge their feelings without judgment but with increased reflections that yield plans to move forward (e.g., journal writing, graphing their behavior on a 1–5 scale).
- Explain the merits of deflecting tension with humor.
- Limit sarcasm; stick to positive comments.
- Know when to react and when not to.

❯ Offer Structured Goals, Parameters, and Resources

Learners with behavioral differences often struggle to understand and follow rules when routines are not predictable or desirable. Consequently, staff need to offer and explain the required structure proactively. This includes announcing changes well in advance; posting daily routines, objectives, and expectations; and highlighting schedule changes and the reasons for the procedures to increase learner buy-in and proactively lessen inappropriate responses. As an example, point out schedule change on a chart or say, "There is no music class today since we have an assembly instead." Reinforce class rules with frequent student and class review. Build in class time to conference with students and open up dialogue.

Resources at your disposal include peers and families. Share daily agendas with families, so they can know, encourage, assist, and reinforce school routines as well as prepare supplies and resources. In addition (and if appropriate), assign and train a peer mentor who—under staff direction and reinforcement—guides a student with daily school/class navigation, routines, learning expectations, and interactions. Realize that older learners may display inappropriate behaviors rather than admit they do not understand a lesson in front of their peers. Parameters include establishing an inviting classroom that encourages learners to ask questions and allows the time for supports and reviews. This minimizes students' anxieties.

❯ Lead with the Positive

Offer praise with realistic, timely, and specific feedback (e.g., cause-effect explanations, videos of themselves that students privately critique to increase self-awareness, positive strides achieved in individualized behavior plans). Be certain to follow district, region, and school policies and procedures regarding parental permission. Notice and reward the small steps toward positive peer engagement and other behaviors. Employ prompts and cues, such as offering a different tone of voice or a nonverbal facial expression. Take the time to model problem-solving skills with behaviors that reflect on the value of persistence to achieve a goal. Offer signals and verbal reminders privately. Value and communicate replacement behaviors. For example, if a learner blurts out an answer and is more impulsive, offer a model of how one waits his or her turn, or suggest a system of jotting down notes instead of calling out.

The goal is to increase strengths by capitalizing on student interests, overshadowing and minimizing the negativity that is all too often affiliated with a classification of emotional disturbance. This requires knowing your students beyond their labels (see appendixes). Highlight learner strengths to compensate for weaker skills. As an example, if a learner has stronger verbal skills or enjoys learning with peers, offer more debate, interactive discussion, and cooperative group work. Find out what a learner likes, and honor those characteristics and preferences. If a student dislikes reading and writing but loves to watch movies, then ask him or her to summarize the plot or compose a critique to increase reading and writing skills. If a student dislikes mathematics, infuse math skills in word problems that include favorite sports figures, popular singers, or vampires, knowing that he or she likes Lionel Messi, Beyoncé, or *Twilight*, respectively.

❥ Respect the Inner Student

Students' outward social, emotional, and behavioral differences do not always reflect their inner thoughts and emotions. Some learners may be good at masking or holding in their true feelings until an incident, interaction, or classroom expectation occurs that invokes what is then labeled as an inappropriate reaction or unexpected behavior.

A sound classroom environment always includes scaffolding for students who need additional attention, nurturing, structure, and proactive support—whether aggression, immaturity, deception, denial, fear, or anxiety is exhibited. Knowing what sort of support to offer means knowing the inner student and imagining how he or she may react to what is perceived as a difficult academic, emotional, behavioral, or social task. You would not administer a math test that involves two- and three-digit numbers if students did not already know how to multiply one-digit factors. Nor would you expect a student to read *The Grapes of Wrath* if he or she were reading on a 4th-grade level. The same holds true with emotional, social, and behavioral interventions; offer appropriate supports in increments that are within a student's capabilities. Vygotsky's zone of proximal development outlines the distance between when a student can perform a task with guidance or instruction and when he or she can solve a problem or complete a task independently (Learning Theories, 2016). The goal should never be to offer instruction on a student's frustration level since the learner will experience higher levels of stress and feelings of incompetence.

Respecting the inner student also means avoiding personal affronts and chastisements in front of peers. Instead, as mentioned, schedule student conferences to review the student's actions individually and in person; offer quiet classroom spaces for behavioral, social, and emotional pauses and reflection (with opportunities for replacement behaviors that redirect unwanted actions); and encourage journal writing, whether in the form of a paragraph, comic dialogue, or hip-hop song. Know the inner student to individualize, support, and respect current and potential levels of social, emotional, and behavioral expression.

● Spin Negative Scenarios into Positive Actions

Validate emotions—do not dismiss student perceptions—but offer behavioral scripts and compensatory strategies to replace negative scenarios and emotions with positive thoughts and activities to diffuse anger (e.g., stress balls, journals to record thoughts, doodling). Describe flexibility versus rigidity in conversations to rehearse appropriate peer interactions, and offer assistance if a student cannot interpret nonverbal communication. Allow students to rate scenarios in degrees of emotional intensity (e.g., an emotional thermometer to deescalate reactions—making an abstract behavior measurable and more concrete, which helps students remain and/or regain calmness). If a student with selective mutism, for example, will not speak in front of his or her peers, then allow that student to write or prerecord a presentation at home or in a smaller setting instead. View the negative as a teachable time that includes alternative choices and reflective decisions for the student.

● Join Forces

Collaborate with school psychologists, guidance counselors, behavioral interventionists, and, as appropriate, outside service providers such as therapists to accurately identify social, emotional, and behavioral differences—as well as possible coexisting conditions. Identification is often tricky, since there is no quantifiable score for these differences as there is for reading level or math proficiency. Screening procedures involve observations and ratings of student behavior. Any subsequent interventions and strategies need to be appropriately leveled, monitored, practiced, transferred, and owned by students, their families, and staff.

Keep in mind that any such intervention or support also has effects on peers and classroom management. If a student has a BIP, keep confrontations unobtrusive and private. Routines and procedures that are not followed need to be replaced with positive behaviors. Be cautious that there is no domino effect on other learners who may imitate the behaviors or avoid contact with the student. Avoid "tug-of-war" conversations that only serve to alienate the student from his or her classmates and authority figures. As an example, do not be baited into reprimanding a student in front of his or her peers and continually pointing out negative behavior. Be a student's "attention ally" and reinforce positive behavior with increased feedback for attention on task.

To sum up this chapter on social, emotional, and behavioral differences, it's important to be an advocate of your students by

- Leading with the positive.
- Validating the student apart from his or her behavior.
- Accepting emotional, social, and behavior differences as a diversity that exists on a student-specific continuum.
- Collaborating with staff, students, peers, and families.
- Believing in student successes with high expectations that are accompanied by step-by-step behavioral plans.
- Sharing smiles.

References

Brownley, B. (2014). Handling a manifestation determination review (MDR). *Wrightslaw*. Available: www.wrightslaw.com/info/discipl.mdr.strategy.htm

Center for Parent Information and Resources. (2015). Emotional disturbance. Available: www.parentcenterhub.org/repository/emotionaldisturbance

Child & Adolescent Psychiatry (2013). Available: www.aacap.org/AACAP/Families_and_Youth/Facts_for_Families/FFF-Guide/Conduct-Disorder-033.aspx

IDEA, Building the Legacy. Available: http://idea.ed.gov/explore/view/p/,root,regs,300,A,300%252E8,

Learning Theories. (2016). Social development theory: Vygotsky. Available: www.learning-theories.com/vygotskys-social-learning-theory.html

U.S. Department of Education, Sec. 300.530, Authority of school personnel. Available: http://idea.ed.gov/explore/view/p/,root,regs,300,E,300%252E530

Professional Resources

American Academy of Child and Adolescent Psychiatry: www.aacap.org

American Psychiatric Association. (2013). *Highlights of changes from DSM-IV-TR to DSM-5*. Washington, DC: Author. Available: www.dsm5.org/Documents/changes%20from%20dsm-iv-tr%20to%20dsm-5.pdf

Building the Legacy: IDEA 2004. Washington, DC: U.S. Department of Education. Available: http://idea.ed.gov/explore/view/p/,root,regs,300,A,300%252E8,c,4,i,

Center for Effective and Collaborative Practices: http://cecp.air.org/promisingpractices/default.asp

Collaborative for Academic, Social, and Emotional Learning: www.casel.org

Depression and Bipolar Support Alliance: www.dbsalliance.org

Do2Learn. (2016). Emotional disturbance: Characteristics: http://do2learn.com/disabilities/CharacteristicsAndStrategies/EmotionalDisturbance_Characteristics.html

Farley, C., Torres, C., Wailehua, C. T., & Cook, L. (2012). Evidence-based practices for students with emotional and behavioral disorders: Improving academic achievement. *Beyond Behavior, 21*(2), 37–43.

International OCD Foundation: https://iocdf.org/about-ocd

Karten, T. (2015). *Inclusion strategies that work! Research-based methods for the classroom* (3rd ed.). Thousand Oaks, CA: Corwin.

Madrigal, S., & Winner, M. G. (2008). *Superflex: A superhero social thinking curriculum*. San Jose, CA: Think Social Publishing.

McCloud, C. (2006). *Have you filled a bucket today? A guide to daily happiness for kids*. Northville, MI: Nelson.

Mental Health America: www.nmha.org

National Alliance on Mental Illness: www.nami.org

National Federation of Families for Children's Mental Health: www.ffcmh.org

National Technical Assistance Center on Positive Behavioral Interventions and Supports: www.pbis.org

The Nonverbal Dictionary, Emotional Cue: www.nonverbal-dictionary.org/2012/12/emotion-cue.html

Selective Mutism Anxiety Research and Treatment Center. (2016). What is selective mutism? Available: www.selectivemutismcenter.org/aboutus/whatisselectivemutism

4
Students with Specific Learning Disabilities (SLDs)

The Possible Whys

Learning disabilities and differences represent the largest category of students who receive special education services. As with other differences, there is no one main cause of a learning disability; there is variability under the specific learning disability (SLD) umbrella. SLD causes may include central nervous system dysfunction, genetic and biological factors, toxins, and medical factors (e.g., premature birth) (NIH, 2014). SLD is often considered a neurological disorder that involves a difference in brain wiring (LDA, n.d.). The definition of specific learning disability in the Individuals with Disabilities Education Act (IDEA) excludes problems primarily caused by hearing, visual, or motor disabilities; intellectual disabilities; emotional disturbance; or economic, cultural, or environmental disadvantage. Dyslexia, discussed separately in this book (see Chapter 1), is the most common learning disability, with causal factors that include differences in brain activity (IDA, n.d.). Physicians use developmental, family, and educational history to make an SLD determination. Schools conduct a comprehensive education evaluation that uses a variety of assessment tools and input from professionals (Morin, 2014). This includes school psychologists, learning consultants, reading and math specialists and interventionists, and both special and general education staff. Family input is also solicited.

IDEA's definition describes SLD as a disorder in psychological processes involved in understanding or using written and/or spoken language that manifests as problems with listening, thinking, speaking, reading, writing, spelling, or doing mathematical calculations (Project IDEAL, 2013; Thurlow et al., 2009). IDEA's definition includes perceptual disabilities, brain injury, minimal brain dysfunction, dyslexia, and developmental aphasia (an inability to speak or understand speech). It affects academic areas and thus can be identified by comparing a student's score on a test of general intelligence with that student's academic achievement or response to evidence-based academic and behavioral interventions.

Evidence-based practice involves research findings based on the systematic collection of data that include observation, experimentation, and the testing of hypotheses with a selection of programs that consistently yield high student achievements (EBBP, 2007; Kretlow & Blatz, 2011). As examples, What Works Clearinghouse (WWC) reports a strong level of supportive evidence of instruction for kindergarteners through 3rd graders that develops an awareness of the segments of sounds in speech and how they link to letters, along with how to decode words and analyze word parts (WWC, 2016). Providing explicit vocabulary instruction and explicit and direct comprehension strategy instruction offers strong evidence of effectiveness for adolescents. This includes repeated exposure to words in multiple contexts, choosing appropriately leveled text, and sharing the strategy implementation with students (Kamil et al., 2008). For mathematics, the What Works Clearinghouse reports strong evidence for systematic mathematical instruction that includes problem-solving models, verbalization of thought processes, guided practice, corrective feedback, and frequent cumulative review (WWC, 2009). Learners with strong social-emotional learning (SEL) achieve higher levels of academic performance, but reliable and valid assessment tools are needed to determine those social-emotional levels (Haggerty, Elgin, & Woolley, 2011).

Response to intervention (RTI) and multitiered systems of support (MTSS) are often used to determine if a student's learning difference results from outside factors, such as the choice of interventions, rather than an innate condition. RTI involves collecting data to identify student levels of performance in academic and behavioral domains. This includes screenings that determine reading, writing, mathematical, and behavioral levels. Progress is monitored and instructional intensity is tiered for interventions that are set up for the whole class, small groups, and individual learners. MTSS includes high-quality, whole-class, and small-group core instruction offered in Tier 1, more intensive instruction given to smaller groups of learners in Tier 2, and more targeted and often highly individualized instruction in Tier 3 in response to data (Gamm, n.d.). If a student does not respond to evidence-based intervention, then an SLD evaluation may result in many states. However, when a student is on the RTI continuum, then that information becomes part of the evaluative data used to determine eligibility (Center for Parent Information and Resources, 2012).

Characteristics and Strengths

Students with SLD often display differences in following routines and directions; demonstrating short- and long-term memory; sustaining attention; completing tasks; learning to read, write, and spell; and doing mathematics. If students exhibit *dyscalculia,* then they have lower number sense and challenges solving math word problems. Students with *dysgraphia* have differences in written expression with the organization of thoughts, spelling, and/or fine-motor tasks. Reading deficits involve decoding, encoding, fluency, and comprehension differences across the disciplines. In addition, social-emotional areas are often affected with lower self-esteem, poor motivation, and difficulties with peer interactions. Again, one SLD characteristic does not necessarily include or exclude another.

Students with specific learning disabilities receive a great disservice if the instruction solely addresses weaker areas or what is identified as a disability or deficit—and does not capitalize on their strengths. A student with a learning disability displays varying levels of reading, writing, math, attention, and perceptual strengths with written and spoken language. A learner with SLD may not excel in math but be an excellent writer, or he or she may have difficulties with reading comprehension but be an excellent musician, artist, speaker, or gymnast—or perhaps he or she has an affinity for theater, dinosaurs, or botany. Instruction that acknowledges these strengths—and is accompanied by individualized interventions that allow learners to absorb concepts and demonstrate their knowledge—is a type of transmediation that values a *can-do* attitude. A learning disability does not disappear as students advance from elementary school to middle school to high school (or to post-secondary settings). Thankfully, neither do the strategies that capitalize on student ability and interventions, which teach each learner to value his or her strengths with models, practice, feedback, and appropriate applications.

Inclusion Strategies
❯ Scaffold, Monitor, Fade

It is vital to help—but not enable—students with SLDs. Lead learners on the road to recognize their level of performance with increased self-advocacy, self-efficacy, metacognition, and plans to move forward. This includes not only acknowledging weaker areas but also—as stated throughout this resource—highlighting and capitalizing on individual learners' strengths. The ultimate goal is for students to accomplish tasks independently, which is possible through individualized and specially designed instruction. Strategies are never generic, since each student with a learning disability is a unique learner.

Appropriate instructional scaffolding is composed of frequent review and repetition, with drill and practice and ongoing monitoring. In other words, a lesson's vocabulary, concepts, and expectations are chunked, modeled, pretaught, dissected, appropriately paced, and presented differently to honor a level of work that challenges but does not frustrate or turn off a student. The emphasis is not on *what* you are teaching but on *how* you are teaching. The content is important, but so is the process. Use ongoing curriculum-based assessments that offer realistic snapshots to guide instruction.

Scaffolding also has learners using tools such as voice-to-text and text-to-voice technology, e-books, or digital pens. Uncluttered worksheets, graphic organizers, and mind maps are different ways to highlight the big ideas of lessons. Graphic organizers and outlines are especially useful in helping students organize and coherently plan thoughts in written expressions. Technology is alternately embraced and viewed as a distraction; however, many digital devices, software, and learning platforms address student diversity and offer options that personalize learning (Herold, 2016). The following sites and apps offer practical visual, auditory, and kinesthetic-tactile tools and strategies to assist students who are capable of learning but who learn differently. Multiple points of access help your students with differences achieve excellence alongside their peers. This list is not exhaustive but includes apps and software that allow a glimpse into the multiple representations and engagements available.

The following tools assist with access to learning and increased conceptual organization, recall, and learner application. These tools are intended to disallow learner differences to inhibit successes. Stated positively, these tools increase understanding and allow multiple forms of engagement and expression for instruction and assessment.

- **Abilipad** (https://appytherapy.com/abilipad/features): Has adaptive writing and reading with features such as a customized keyboard, text to speech, and a word prediction program.
- **Animoto** (https://animoto.com): Videos are created with photos, video clips, songs, and text.
- **Audio Note** (http://luminantsoftware.com/iphone/audionote.html): Class notes and audio are linked, organized, highlighted, and better remembered.
- **Brainpop** (www.brainpop.com, www.brainpopjr.com): Content includes animated movies on topics in English, mathematics, science, social studies, health, art, music, and technology with accompanying interactive quizzes,

games, and activities for access on computers and mobile devices. (Also available in Spanish and French.)

- **CAST UDL Book Builder** (http://bookbuilder.cast.org): Site to create, read, share, and publish digital books.
- **Dragon Dictation** (www.nuance.com/for-individuals/mobile-applications/dragon-dictation/index.htm): Voice dictates text in word documents, tweets, emails, Facebook posts, and so on.
- **Enchanted Learning** (www.enchantedlearning.com/Home.html): Educational website with K–12 learning activities across the disciplines.
- **Evernote** (https://evernote.com): Allows pictures and written thoughts to be captured, saved, tagged, and accessed from multiple devices.
- **Flocabulary Educational Hip Hop** (www.flocabulary.com): Academic content is translated into hip-hop songs with accompanying lessons in history, language arts, science, social studies, math, vocabulary, current events, and life skills.
- **Freeology Graphic Organizers** (http://freeology.com): Graphic organizers across subject areas are accessed.
- **Funbrain** (www.funbrain.com): Online educational games are navigated to explore reading, math, and critical thinking skills.
- **Glogster** (http://edu.glogster.com): Interactive multimedia posters for design and access.
- **GoAnimate** (http://goanimate.com): Platform to create animated videos to communicate messages and concepts using avatars as characters with scripted voice recordings.
- **Good Reader** (www.goodreader.com): PDF reader for iPad and iPhone to read, copy, annotate, create, and manage documents, files, and movies.
- **Inspiration Software** (www.inspiration.com): Graphic organizers, outlines, and diagrams accompanied by visuals arrange big curriculum ideas, details, academic vocabulary, and concepts. Kidspiration is specifically for Grades K–5 (www.inspiration.com/Kidspiration).
- **Kahoot** (https://kahoot.it): Online learning environment with subject-related questions/quizzes, discussions, and surveys to access and create.
- **Khan Academy** (www.khanacademy.org): Step-by-step online instructional videos that students access to increase their learning across the disciplines and K–12 grades—from algebra to economics, art history, and more.
- **Live Scribe** (www.livescribe.com/en-us): Smartpen that assists with note taking to capture what is heard and written, and has the ability to play back words, diagrams, symbols, and audio.

- **Mind Mapping** (www.mindmapping.com): Visual organization and diagramming of thoughts and information with the main ideas branching out to details on a given topic using both words and pictures.
- **Notability** (www.gingerlabs.com): Project management for notes, photos, and sketches that are created, organized, annotated, emailed, and exported to Dropbox.
- **Phonics Genius** (http://dyslexiahelp.umich.edu/tools/apps/phonics-genius-free): App that helps younger learners increase phonemic awareness to speak, read, and recognize words through their sounds.
- **Plickers** (https://plickers.com): Assessment tool that offers real-time data on student progress with a quick teacher scan of responses to online questions.
- **Popplet iPad Tool** (http://popplet.com): iPad app that organizes concepts into visual outlines to see the relationships between broader topics and details.
- **Quizlet** (https://quizlet.com): Online site with study skill sets of flashcards that are created and accessed by students and educators and that contain vocabulary and definitions offered across the disciplines. Learning activities and games correspond to the vocabulary sets. Has text to voice feature and options to include images.
- **Scribblit** (http://scribblitt.com): *S*elf-publishing site where learners pick their own characters, stories, and illustrations to create and share stories.
- **Super Teacher Tools** (www.superteachertools.com): Instructional, management, and organizational tools for teachers with review games such as *Jeopardy* and *Who Wants to Be a Millionaire,* seating charts, timers, group makers, and QR codes.
- **Voice Dream Reader** (www.voicedream.com): Voice-based mobile and app that turns text from books, articles, and documents into speech read aloud.
- **VisuWords** (www.visuwords.com): Online graphical dictionary that visually associates and connects vocabulary with definitions, related words, and additional concepts.
- **Wordle** (www.wordle.net): Creation of word clouds from text that highlights the main ideas with images of the arranged words.
- **Zunal** (http://zunal.com): Site to create and access curriculum related to K–12 webquests in art, music, business, economics, language arts, health, physical education, life skills, careers, science, mathematics, social studies, and technology.

Monitoring a student's progress will help you know when to begin gradually decreasing—or fading—the use of your scaffolding supports. An educator in a recent professional development session related that her favorite teaching moment was when one of her students, a junior in high school, told her that although he liked her support as a resource teacher throughout his high school years, her services would no longer be needed. This statement affirmed that the learning strategies now belonged to this young man, not the teacher.

❯ Concretize the Abstract

Students with SLD learn but in different ways. Continually consider ways to allow abstract concepts to become concrete, generalized, and—ultimately—understood. Presenting manipulatives and alternative formats allows learners to circumvent perceptual difficulties if they see, hear, and interpret input differently. Offer universal design for learning (UDL) principles. UDL is a framework that is intended to allow the curriculum to be accessible to all learners through multiple means of representation, action and expression, and engagement (CAST, 2015). With UDL, diversified goals, methods, materials, and assessments become routine practice—rather than the exception. Infuse visual, auditory, and kinesthetic approaches that allow learners to see, hear, feel, and experience what might otherwise be viewed as an abstract or foreign concept. Hearing an abstract concept includes listening to a hip-hop song about the Bill of Rights, hearing a digital recording of *A Raisin in the Sun,* or activating the text-to-speech feature on a website when reading a nonfiction article.

Jean Piaget theorized that in the concrete operational stage of development, students achieve deductive and inductive reasoning through generalizations, along with trial and error to develop more abstract thought (McLeod, 2009). As examples, an early-grade student may not understand that a set of five objects is greater than a set of three objects until he or she repeatedly counts sets of objects—be they a collection of chips, crayons, or coins. A student studying the ancient Mesopotamian civilization is enlivened when viewing, touching, and creating replicas of Sumerian statuettes or imitating cuneiform by scribing on clay tablets. A student with a reading difference, such as dyslexia, may prefer to tap out or clap each syllable to understand the parts of multisyllabic words rather than just read the text. Learners who use two differently colored skeins of yarn to demonstrate lines of latitude and longitude absorb the concept more than just looking at a map in the textbook. Instruction includes guided practice and attention to learner responses to visual, auditory, and tactile stimuli. Let the manipulatives chosen assist and enhance instruction.

❯ Teach Real-Life Literacy and Math Applications

Anchor instruction to real-life applications to allow reading, writing, and mathematics to exist beyond a workbook or text page. Literacy and math skills are also life skills. As examples, reading newspapers keeps students in touch with their communities, countries, and global events, while they simultaneously help students decode, expand vocabulary, and both comprehend and infer salient points of view. Literacy skills are also gained while reading a recipe in a cookbook or an online kids' cooking site such as Spatulatta (www.spatulatta.com). Hone students' reading skills with to-do lists, advertisements, labels, and signs around the classroom and school. Encourage families to continue the real-life reading experience at shopping malls, on family trips, or with grocery lists, phone bills, credit card statements, online maps, and game directions.

Writing skills also have real-life applicability, with examples being Facebook posts, texts, tweets, thank-you cards, labels for classroom objects, personal narratives, and editorials. Even though Facebook posts, tweets, and texts often use slang and shorthand, they are part of a student's reality. A valuable and interest-based writing lesson could involve students comparing and contrasting these forms of writing to standards-based English, which should increase metacognition as similarities and differences among the diverse forums are noted. In addition, math calculations surface in everyday actions such as preparing a budget, figuring out a restaurant tip, measuring the distance between two places on a map, determining how to slice a pizza so everyone gets an equally sized piece, noticing geometric patterns in a shirt or dress design, or calculating a baseball player's batting average. Enliven instruction by using real-life math and literacy contexts such as these in homework problems, classroom instruction, and quizzes.

❯ Strengthen Memory and Metacognition

Memory affects our ability to learn information, retain it, and use it later (Learning Disabilities Association of America, n.d.). What we call *memory* consists of working memory, short-term memory, and long-term memory—respectively, holding on to information, using it for temporary retrieval, and then retaining the information for longer periods of time. Often, memory is enhanced and strengthened through sensory input (visual, auditory, or tactile means). The process of acoustic, visual, and tactile encoding allows memories to be respectively processed and stored by sound, images, and touch, which are later recalled from short- or long-term memory (Mastin, 2010). Mastin speaks about semantic encoding that interprets the sensory input within context and then creates association to derive more meaning.

In this age of information overload, students are able to access an incredible amount of information, but they do not always remember, retain, retrieve, and apply what they learn. Mnemonics and acrostics offer students with learning differences an easy way to retrieve information. Of course, learners need to expand that information with repeated exposure and more follow-ups, but these tools can help the learning wheels keep turning. During a science lesson, a student once told me that he used *www.erosion* to stand for *wind, water,* and *weathering.* We had been practicing and using acrostics, but this was one that he had designed as his own study tool to strengthen his memory of the concept, heightening his awareness of how to learn.

The following acrostic describes this awareness, which is known as *metacognition*:

Mastery requires reflection.

Efficacy levels are raised when errors are spun into learning opportunities.

Thinking about thinking moves students forward.

Awareness of what is known and needs to be known is increased.

Changes occur in thought processes.

Ongoing self-evaluation yields improvements.

Giving realistic feedback means being attuned to the strategies.

Neurocognitive function improves.

Involvement in the strategies means accepting challenge as growth.

Time to process and reflect is essential.

Instruction increases access to active participation.

One knows, regulates, and sets learning goals.

Needing help involves recognizing your weaker skills and then leveraging the appropriate strategies to strengthen them.

⊙ Empower Peers

Peer mentors, who are the same age or older, can be role models who offer help without the embarrassment of an adult hovering over the student. Consider setting up an ongoing system with peers as mentors, such as reciprocal reading, classwide peer tutoring, or cooperative problem solving. Be sure to clearly explain the roles of the mentor and mentee, and offer ongoing training, supervision, and support.

Just as specially designed instruction is individualized, so are peer mentoring programs. The benefits can include increased learner knowledge, greater academic achievement, higher self-esteem, deeper engagement, and positive social behaviors (Irvin, Meltzer, & Dukes, 2007).

❯ Be a Team Player

If students have difficulties with decoding, fluency, and comprehension, then seek out reading specialists and instructional reading coaches for assistance. Often, speech-language pathologists can offer additional tips and resources to help students with dyslexia. Basic skills teachers and math interventionists can teach lessons to the whole class, small groups, and individual students. Coteachers can offer parallel lessons to teach similar concepts at different paces and/or levels of engagement. During a lesson on the parts of speech, for example, one teacher can ask a group of students to highlight nouns and adjectives in a text, while another teacher helps a group create diamantes or diagram sentences.

Be a team player with all staff on board—not only general and special education teachers and related staff but also administrators, instructional assistants, school secretaries, librarians, interns, volunteers, and all members of the school community —to get additional insights and expertise before, during, and after instruction and assessments. Teams should also be composed of the students themselves and their families. Even though families of students with learning disabilities and other differences are at various levels of acceptance—with some experiencing frustration, denial, and even hostility—communication is vital. Collaborative planning occurs not only during parent-teacher conferences or at back-to-school night but also at football games, school dances, and community activities. Get to know your students and their families so you can capitalize on opportunities outside school and share ideas with one another.

To sum up this chapter on specific learning disabilities, it's important to be an advocate of your students by

- Acknowledging current learner levels with appropriate scaffolding and supports.
- Offering help without enabling.
- Knowing when to fade support.
- Implementing different pacing with repetition and enrichment.
- Having high expectations.
- Encouraging, coaching, guiding, and praising.
- Strengthening memory.
- Making real-life literacy and mathematical connections.
- Empowering students' peers as mentors.
- Being a team member.

References

Center for Applied and Special Technology. (2015). About universal design for learning. Wakefield, MA. Available: www.cast.org/our-work/about-udl.html

Center for Parent Information and Resources. (2012). Response to Intervention. Available: www.parentcenterhub.org/repository/rti

Evidence-Based Behavioral Practice. (2007). Defining evidence-based behavioral practice. Available: http://ebbp.org/ebbp.html

Gamm, S. (n.d.). RTI-based SLD identification toolkit: Cautions when using an RTI-SLD identification toolkit. RTI Action Network. Available: www.rtinetwork.org/getstarted/sld-identification-toolkit/ld-identification-toolkit-cautions

Haggerty, K., Elgin, J., & Woolley, A. (2011). Social emotional-learning assessment measures for middle school youth. Raikes Foundation. Available: www.search-kinstitute.org/sites/default/files/a/DAP-Raikes-Foundation-Review.pdf

Herold, B. (2016). Technology in education: An overview. *Education Review*. Available: www.edweek.org/ew/issues/technology-in-education/

International Dyslexia Association. (n.d.). Dyslexia and the brain: https://dyslexiaida.org/dyslexia-and-the-brain-fact-sheet

Irvin, J., Meltzer, J, & Dukes, M. (2007). *Taking action on adolescent literacy*. Alexandria, VA: ASCD.

Kamil, M. L., Borman, G. D., Dole, J., Kral, C. C., Salinger, T., & Torgesen, J. (2008). *Improving adolescent literacy: Effective classroom and intervention practices: A Practice Guide* (NCEE #2008-4027). Washington, DC: National Center for Education Evaluation and Regional Assistance, Institute of Education Sciences, U.S. Department of Education. Available: http://ies.ed.gov/ncee/wwc

Kretlow, A., & Blatz, S. (2011). The ABCs of evidence-based practice for teachers. *Teaching Exceptional Children, 43*(5), 8–19.

Learning Disabilities Association of America. (n.d.). https://ldaamerica.org/support/new-to-ld

Mastin, L. (2010). Memory encoding. *The Human Memory*. Available: www.human-memory.net/processes_encoding.html

McLeod, S. (2009). Jean Piaget. *Simply Psychology*. Available: www.simplypsychology.org/piaget.html

Morin, A. (2014). Understanding the full evaluation process, Understood for Learning and Attention Issues. Available: www.understood.org/en/school-learning/evaluations/evaluation-basics/understanding-the-full-evaluation-process

National Institutes of Health. (2014). What causes learning disabilities? *Eunice Kennedy Shriver National Institute of Child Health and Human Development*. Available: www.nichd.nih.gov/health/topics/learning/conditioninfo/pages/causes.aspx

Project IDEAL. (2013). Specific learning disabilities. Available: www.projectidealonline.org/v/specific-learning-disabilities

Thurlow, M. L., Moen, R. E., Liu, K. K., Scullin, S., Hausmann, K. E., & Shyyan, V. (2009). *Disabilities and reading: Understanding the effects of disabilities and their relationship to reading instruction and assessment*. Minneapolis: University of Minnesota, Partnership for Accessible Reading Assessment.

What Works Clearinghouse. (2009). Students struggling with mathematics: Response to intervention (RtI) for elementary and middle schools. Available: http://ies.ed.gov/ncee/wwc/practiceguide.aspx?sid=2

What Works Clearinghouse. (2016). Foundational skills to support reading for understanding in kindergarten through 3rd grade. Available: http://ies.ed.gov/ncee/wwc/PracticeGuide.aspx?sid=21

Professional Resources

A to Z of Brain, Mind and Learning: www.learninginfo.org/acrostics.htm

Building the legacy: IDEA 2004. Washington, DC: U.S. Department of Education. Available: http://idea.ed.gov/explore/view/p/,root,statute,I,A,602,30

CAST: About Universal Design for Learning: www.cast.org/our-work/about-udl.html#.VwRf-ou05q4

Center for Neurological and Neurodevelopment Health: www.cnnh.org

Collaborative for Academic, Social, and Emotional Learning (CASEL): www.casel.org

Dyscalculia: www.dyscalculia.org

Eye to Eye: www.eyetoeyenational.org

Hott, B., & Walker, J. (2012). Peer tutoring. *Council for Learning Disabilities*. Available: www.council-for-learning-disabilities.org/peer-tutoring-flexible-peer-mediated-strategy-that-involves-students-serving-as-academic-tutors

Hughes, C., & Dexter, D. (n.d.). The use of RTI to identify students with learning disabilities: A review of the research. *RTI Action Network*. Available: www.rtinetwork.org/learn/research/use-rti-identify-students-learning-disabilities-review-research

International Dyslexia Association: www.interdys.org

LD Online: www.ldonline.org

Learning Disabilities Association of America. (2016). Types of learning disabilities. Available: https://ldaamerica.org/types-of-learning-disabilities/memory

Metcalf, T. (n.d.). What's your plan? Accurate decision making within a multi-tiered system of supports: Critical areas in tier 1. *RTI Action Network*. Available: www.rtinetwork.org/essential/tieredinstruction/tier1/accurate-decision-making-within-a-multi-tier-system-of-supports-critical-areas-in-tier-1

National Center for Learning Disabilities: http://ncld.org

Patino, E. (2014). How having mentors can help kids with learning and attention issues. *Understood*. Available: www.understood.org/en/friends-feelings/empowering-your-child/self-esteem/how-having-mentors-can-help-kids-with-learning-and-attention-issues

The Strategic Instruction Model, University of Kansas: http://sim.kucrl.org

Teaching LD: www.dldcec.org

Undertood.org. (2014). Understanding dysgraphia. Available: www.understood.org/en/learning-attention-issues/child-learning-disabilities/dysgraphia/understanding-dysgraphia

5

Students with Executive Function (EF) Disorder

The Possible Whys

Executive functions reference cognitive skills that affect organization and regulation (UCSF, 2016). These skills include but are not limited to attention, planning, problem solving, self-regulation, decision making, and the ability to concentrate on relevant sensory information. The exact cause of executive function (EF) disorder is unknown. It has been linked to disease or injury to the frontal lobe of the brain, which adversely affects a student's ability to carry out a task, handle daily routines, and anticipate consequences (Headway, 2016). Studies indicate that genes and heredity may also be factors (Morin, n.d.), as EF disorder is evidenced within families, and some learners are born with fragile or weak executive function. In addition, EF disorder is often displayed with other differences (e.g., specific learning disabilities, emotional differences, autism, attention deficit hyperactivity disorder [ADHD], acquired brain injury).

Characteristics and Strengths

Executive function has been likened to the conductor of an orchestra who allows the diverse musicians to be heard (Packer, n.d.). As the so-called CEO of the brain (Morin, n.d.), executive function is ultimately the one in charge. In EF disorder, unless direction is explicitly outlined, a disconnect in delegating task responsibilities—which help us know the next steps—is sometimes elusive. Such a disconnect occurs from missed directions, faulty signals, and weak information transmissions and misinterpretations, which thereby results in inaccurate task completion and often a frustrated, confused, and overwhelmed student. For example, if a teacher mentions that there is an upcoming homework assignment, a learner does not follow through by writing this communication in an assignment pad. Even if the assignment was recorded, a learner may not remember to take the necessary actions to look at the pad and then complete the assignment by the given due date or within the parameters outlined. Learner questions are not clarified, because they are often not voiced. Sometimes a student's silence may not indicate understanding but stem from not knowing which question to ask.

Students with EF disorder exhibit difficulties carrying out daily tasks. Assessments and screenings to identify EF disorder include neuropsychological tests, observations, interviews, and rating scales. The Behavior Rating Inventory of Executive Function is a questionnaire for parents and teachers to assess executive function behaviors of students 5 to 18 years old in school and home environments (Guy, Isquith, & Gioia, 2000). Topics surveyed include emotional control, inhibitory behaviors, and the ability to switch between activities, along with organization, planning, and working memory.

Signs and symptoms of EF are evidenced with differences in the following skills:

- Attending to and analyzing tasks to extract vital information.
- Initiating and completing assignments.
- Managing time to organize the discrete steps of presented tasks.
- Pacing assignments and responsibilities.
- Juggling deadlines (e.g., starting a long-term assignment the night before its due date).
- Organizing and acting on verbal and written information.
- Sequencing thoughts and actions.
- Remembering and applying information.
- Shifting from one activity or assignment to the next.
- Changing course if the initial plan is not working.
- Completing class and homework assignments.
- Multitasking.
- Seeking help from peers and adults.
- Researching information.
- Using impulse control.
- Setting future goals.

It is important to note that there is a range of symptoms—with some more overt or subtle than others. Since multitasking and motivation are often affected, it is important that staff recognize the individuality of each learner. This includes noting learner strengths, interests, and preferences. If a learner has strong computer skills, then offering him or her a digital calendar or the opportunity to use an appropriate app is a wise way to acknowledge that student's strength to circumvent his or her weaker organizational skills. If a learner with EF disorder has stronger interpersonal skills, then enlisting a peer mentor to model and monitor class routines is also a viable choice.

Classroom Implications

Schools have ongoing daily expectations that can overwhelm and frustrate students with EF disorder, owing to their limited organization skills, poor memory, distractibility, weaker impulse control, and lower planning skills. In response, staff members need to hone their own executive skills and offer students appropriate levels of support. For example, handing out a long-term project with a schedule and calendar with due dates highlighted is helpful for students with EF disorder. The teacher should also intermittently monitor the students' steps toward completing that assignment. Hence, the responsibility lies with both the teacher and the students to organize, plan, and accept supportive strategies. In addition, it's important to involve families in the plan, so all messages and instructional approaches are universally shared.

Inclusion Strategies

❯ Help Students Set Goals

Invite students to set goals, plan, sequence, and pace their work. Ultimately, we want students to increase their self-awareness so they set their own goals that increase academic, behavioral, emotional, and social skills for accurate task completion. This goal setting includes establishing improvement plans to better sequence, prioritize, initiate, organize, and follow through with the skills necessary to honor expectations. A step-by-step approach casts the teacher as a coach who encourages and monitors students in order to gauge progress and help them overcome obstacles.

❯ Offer Organizational Models

Once goals are set, an organized plan for the execution of these goals should come next. At times, organization includes changing the physical or social environment and adding or removing visual or auditory cues (Center on Brain Injury Research and Training, n.d.). The environment can offer assistance, but sometimes it also presents distractions that students with executive function disorder may not be able to filter out. Sometimes offering too much direction will confuse a student since he or she is not given sufficient time to process and reflect on the task requirements. A student seated near a window or an open door may become distracted by visual and auditory stimuli. In addition, sitting near peers who can be organizational mentors, rather than those who are disorganized accomplices, is obviously helpful.

Organizational supports include dividing a task into parts and then monitoring steps toward completion. Longer tasks often need to be reworded or accompanied by pictures. The example shown in Figure 5.1 is one way to help students be certain that they complete all parts of a book report assignment. The components are outlined with a checklist that serves as a self-monitoring plan to increase planning skills. Figures 5.2 and 5.3 are alternative formats for the same assignment, but they use less text. Students with weaker EF skills may perceive these options as more attractive. Review these models to reexamine how you organize and present written requirements for your class's assignments.

❯ Promote Attention and Retention

Infuse your presentations with kinesthetic (movement) opportunities to maximize attention and minimize distractibility. If there is a lot of information to remember, then encourage students to create mnemonics or acrostics, chunk information, or associate one word or sentence to a concept to strengthen their working memory. The more creative the memory device, the more likely students' attention will remain high and their memory enhanced. As an example, a student who uses "*My* very *e*ducated *m*other *j*ust *s*erved *u*s *n*achos" to remember the planets' order from the sun can more readily incorporate this information in the answer to an essay question about the solar system. To add a kinesthetic element, assign a different planet to eight students and then ask them to stand in the correct order in front of another learner who represents the sun. To add a tactile element, and to organize and solidify facts, students can create 3D replicas from clay, Styrofoam, or crumbled paper to represent the varying mass, diameter, and density of each planet. To add both visual and interpersonal elements, groups of three or four students can "jigsaw" the eight planets, as each group researches a planet and then creates a presentation or oral report. The groups then combine their respective work into a whole-class presentation on the solar system. Diverse multimodal instruction such as this science example helps solidify concepts for a student who has weaker retention and attention.

❯ Monitor Behaviors

Perform frequent notebook and desk checks to ensure that workspaces and student folders are organized and complete. Encourage students to self-monitor by using a diary of work completed on paper or digital calendars (daily, weekly, or monthly) to increase the executive function of organization skills. Address impulsivity with private reminders, and employ student self-regulation to record appropriate behaviors (e.g., daily tallying of time on task, appropriate class participation, effective peer interactions during cooperative work.) See Figure 5.4 for a sample behavioral

Figure 5.1 | Book Report Assignment

My Book Report (Fiction)

Part 1: Written Report

1. The title page has:
- ☐ my name
- ☐ the title of the book
- ☐ the author
- ☐ illustrator (if there is one)
- ☐ the type of fiction:
- ☐ realistic, adventure, fantasy, historical, biographical, horror, science fiction…

2. I included a description of the setting: (3–5 sentences)
- ☐ when the story happened
- ☐ where the story happened

3. I communicated information about the main characters: (3–5 sentences)
- ☐ physical description (age, appearance)
- ☐ personality traits with all of these included:
  - ☐ actions attitudes ☐ behaviors ☐ book/chapter example

4. I shared information about the author's point of view (choose ONE):
- ☐ a. first person–character as narrator (uses words such as *I, me, my, we, our*)
- ☐ b. third person–someone else tells the story (uses words *as he, she, they, his, her*)
- ☐ c. mixed narration (point of view is shared from multiple characters/voices)

5. I included a summary of the plot in 8–10 sentences that includes ALL of these:
- ☐ a. problem
- ☐ b. rising action
- ☐ c. solution
- ☐ d. favorite part

Part 2: Project

I select ONE of these projects: (highlight choice)

a picture of a favorite scene with a caption that describes the picture	a song from the point of view of one of the main characters or the narrator	a display with information about the characters, setting, plot, rising action, and ending	a slide presentation (at least six slides) about the characters, setting, plot, and resolution	an advertisement for the book that offers reasons why or why not someone should read it	a poem (in the style of a favorite poet) that tells the plot of the story

- ☐ I did not understand part of this book or assignment, so I asked for help.
- ☐ I achieved excellent results because I followed step-by-step instructions.
- ☐ I read my book each day and took notes.
- ☐ Other comments _____

Figure 5.2 | Fiction Book Report

My Book Report (Fiction)				
A. Title Page	B. Setting	C. Characters	D. Point of View	E. Summary
☐ my name ☐ the title of the book ☐ the author ☐ illustrator (if there is one) ☐ the type of fiction: realistic, adventure, fantasy, historical, biographical, horror, science fiction, etc.	I included a description of the <u>setting:</u> (3–5 sentences) ☐ when the story happened ☐ where the story happened	I communicated information about the <u>main characters:</u> (3–5 sentences) ☐ physical description (age, appearance) ☐ personality traits with all of these included: *actions, attitudes, behaviors, book/chapter example*	I shared information about the author's point of view (choose ONE): ☐ a. first-person narrator (uses words such as *I, me, my, we, our*) ☐ b. third-person narrator (uses words such as *he, she, they, his, her*) ☐ c. mixed narration (point of view is shared from multiple characters/voices)	I included a summary of the plot in 8–10 sentences that includes ALL of these: ☐ a. problem ☐ b. rising action ☐ c. solution ☐ d. favorite part

Figure 5.3 | Book Report Assignment Options

PICTURE of a favorite scene with a caption that describes the picture	SONG from the point of view of one of the main characters or the narrator	DISPLAY with information about the characters, setting, plot, rising action, and ending	SLIDE PRESENTATION (at least six slides) about the characters, setting, plot, and resolution	ADVERTISEMENT for the book that offers reasons why or why not someone should read it	POEM (in the style of a favorite poet) that tells the plot of the story

rating scale. Finally, keep the language on classroom charts used to monitor behavior simple and direct, and accompany it with clear verbal reminders.

To sum up this chapter on executive function disorder, it's important to be an advocate of your students by

- Being a planning partner.
- Having a role as a time coach, not an exclusive timekeeper.
- Overseeing organization with timely feedback.
- Observing and documenting executive behavior.
- Offering, explaining, and monitoring consistent usage of strategies and resources.

- Sharing progress toward task completion.
- Increasing learner reflection and ownership.
- Revisiting the plan.
- Acknowledging executive diversity as a difference, not a willful decision.
- Providing opportunities to experience success.

Figure 5.4 | Behavioral Rating Scale

I completed the assignment accurately.		
Not at All	Partly	Perfect!
1 2 3	4 5 6	7 8 9 10
I learned that _____ .		

References

Center on Brain Injury Research and Training. (n.d.) Available: http://cbirt.org/tbi-education/executive-functions/classroom-interventions-executive-functions/

Guy, S. C., Isquith, P. K., & Gioia, G. A. (2000). *The behavior rating inventory of executive function: Self-report version.* Lutz, FL: Psychological Assessment Resources.

Headway. (2016). Executive dysfunction after brain injury. Available: www.headway.org.uk/about-brain-injury/individuals/effects-of-brain-injury/executive-dysfunction

Morin, A. (n.d.) Understanding executive functioning issues. *Understood.* Available: www.understood.org/en/learning-attention-issues/child-learning-disabilities/executive-functioning-issues/understanding-executive-functioning-issues

Packer, L. (n.d.) Overview of executive dysfunction. Available: www.schoolbehavior.com/disorders/executive-dysfunction/overview-of-executive-dysfunction

University of California–San Francisco. (2016). Executive functions. Available: http://memory.ucsf.edu/ftd/overview/biology/executive/single

Professional Resources

Center on the Developing Child. (2016). Executive function & self-regulation. Available: http://developingchild.harvard.edu/science/key-concepts/executive-function/

Elliott, R. (2003). Executive functions and their disorders. *British Medical Bulletin, 65*(1), 49–59. Available: http://bmb.oxfordjournals.org/content/65/1/49.full

Hansen, S. (2013). *The executive functioning workbook for teens: Help for unprepared, late, and scattered teens.* Champaign, IL: Research Press.

Silver, L. (2006). Is it executive function disorder or ADHD? *ADDitide Online Magazine.* Available: www.additudemag.com/adhd/article/7051.html

6

Students with Speech and Language Disorders

The Possible Whys

Speech offers an expression of thoughts that convey meaning through language. When Prince Albert became King George VI in 1936, he feared that his stuttering would negatively affect his regal voice, but his stammering did not define him, as he went on to deliver live radio broadcasts and speak at public appearances (Stuttering Foundation, 2016). His speech therapist offered him breathing exercises and difficult phrases to practice. Whether the cause was physical or psychological, the lesson learned was that the etiology underlying his speech difficulties did not define his success. Speech and language disorders have multiple causes, which range from medical problems to unknown reasons (American Speech-Language-Hearing Association [ASHA], 2016). Some articulation problems are due to differences in muscles and bones (e.g., cleft palate, teeth misalignment). The causes of voice disorders include but are not limited to polyps, cysts, overuse, and stomach acid (U.S. National Library of Medicine, n.d.). Childhood apraxia of speech is related to impairment in fetal development or is caused by an infection or injury before or after birth. Dysarthria—which is slow or slurred speech, and speech that is often hard to understand—is attributed to tongue and muscle weakness and to neurological disorders that include brain tumors, brain injury, strokes, and facial paralysis. Learners can also exhibit speech and language disorders and severe phonological disorders that result from another condition, such as intellectual disability, hearing loss, cerebral palsy, and autism. Some speech and language disorders are hereditary and occur in families.

Characteristics and Strengths

Speech disorders include voice problems and difficulty articulating speech sounds, speaking with flow or fluency, and comprehending and using language for oral communication and understanding. Language disorders are receptive and/or expressive, which affects students' ability to understand and share thoughts, respectively. Speech and language disorders also spill over to differences in reading, writing, and listening. These range from learning the appropriate sounds of letters to using vocabulary in speech; writing an essay; listening to and extracting information from class instruction; giving an oral presentation; working in cooperative groups; and interacting with peers on the bus, in the lunchroom, and in other settings.

Differing levels of speech may lead to embarrassment and frustration. A learner with dysfluency (stuttering) who exhibits speech interruptions and repeats words or hesitates to speak, or a student who speaks too loudly or softly, can have difficulties with peer and adult conversations. It is important to realize that students who have speech differences are often just as capable academically as other students, despite their communication and language differences. As with other differences, it's critical to tap into each learner's interests and strengths to remediate his or her weaker communication and language skills (see Appendix A).

Classroom Implications

A teacher is a role model whose use of language facilitates communication. If a student has a speech-related service listed in his or her individualized education program (IEP), then instruction may occur in a variety and combination of locations and environments that include pull-out settings, general education classrooms, and online services.

Collaborate with the speech-language pathologist (SLP) who provides speech and language therapy in school as a related service under the Individuals with Disabilities Education Act (IDEA). Under the SLP's auspices, IEP speech goals are transferred to functional-naturalistic settings, including the classroom. Educators are collaborative partners who help learners hone skills across the curriculum, meeting state requirements, asking questions, speaking to peers, decoding words, reading, writing, and communicating purposefully and effectively in a nonthreatening environment.

Inclusion Strategies

❍ Set Up Communication Profiles

Communication profiles describe verbal and nonverbal communications—smiles, head nods, interactions with peers or teachers, and daily classroom routines. They consider receptive and expressive language skills that include words, gestures, ways to follow directions, self-expression, voice quality, and the appropriateness of the communication. A communication profile, also referred to as a communication dictionary or inventory, documents the ways that a person communicates and how others communicate with him or her (Bruce, 2010; Temple University, 2016).

In school settings, a profile is designed to increase knowledge of a student's communication with everyone in the building, including all staff members, specialists, substitute teachers, lunchroom aides, and peers. Language and speech patterns, vocabulary choices, triggers, speech-language behaviors and preferences, and rate of progress are noted. Profiles are intended to encourage participation and independence and to celebrate language successes. Receptive and expressive communicative forms, such as verbalizations, body language, gestures, signs, and speech generating devices (SGD), are outlined. A communication profile is intended to describe and inventory a student's level and communication preference. This in turn leads to increased understanding, recognition, and validation with appropriate interventions. Some students in certain disability categories need to be taught appropriate communications to express a variety of emotions and needs that include anxiety, hunger, anger, and both happiness and frustrations with academic and social expectations and interactions.

❍ Determine, Support, and Monitor

Students display different speech-language levels, and it's important to identify them before interventions are selected. As with all differences, the specially designed instruction corresponds to unique student characteristics and profiles. The following sections describe how you can screen, support, and monitor for phonology, morphology, syntax, semantics, and pragmatics. These refer, respectively, to speech-sound rules, word structure, sentence structure, vocabulary and word meanings, and language in social situations such as conversation.

Phonology: Speech-Sound Rules

If a student has difficulties with phonology or speech-sound rules, then it's a good idea to frequently use informal phonics inventories to note patterns and drive instruction. For example, ask the student to identify, pronounce, and sound out letters, vowel combinations, consonant clusters, and blends in the initial, medial, and final positions (i.e., the speech sounds at the start, middle, and end of a word). Record types of speech-sound and articulation errors: deletions, omissions, substitutions, distortions, and additions in passages read aloud. Be certain students demonstrate decoding (reading) and encoding (spelling) skills with real and made-up words to ensure that they are learning to break the phonetic code—not just memorizing words. As an example, if you are teaching medial short vowel sounds, have students read a list of words such as *cat, bed, pig, hot,* and *cup* along with a list of nonsense words such as *dat, zed, tig, bot,* and *rup.*

Morphology: Word Structure

If a student has difficulties with morphology (word organization, parts of speech, and word structure), then speak clearly and slowly and explain how words are formed. Offer lists of curriculum-related nouns, verbs, adjectives, and adverbs that emphasize the similarities and differences of words, along with prefixes and suffixes. Figure 6.1 offers a model for how to visually assist learners to better organize and recognize different parts of speech centered on a curriculum area in social studies—in this case, government.

Figure 6.1 | Government Words: Related Parts of Speech

Our Government			
Noun	**Verb**	**Adjective**	**Adverb**
government	govern	governmental	governmentally
representative	represent	representable, representative	
nation		national	nationally
power	empower	powerful	powerfully
president	preside	presidential	presidentially
democracy		democratic	democratically

Syntax: Sentence Structure

If a student has difficulties with syntax or sentence structure, then ask him or her to read various examples of prose and poetry with appropriate inflections, elaboration, and sequencing of thoughts. Give students opportunities to reorganize the words and clauses in sentences. This can be as simple as rearranging words written on index cards to reinforce the difference between a statement and a question (see Figure 6.2). This exercise can then lead to a lesson on inflection, capitalization, and punctuation.

Figure 6.2 | Index Cards to Practice Syntax

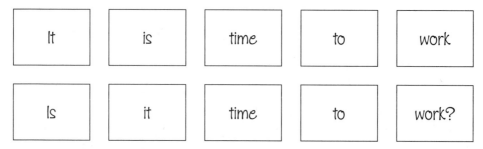

Use written and oral interventions to practice and reinforce skills with both sentence structure and prepositional phrases that offer personal connections and subject connections. For example, if using daily oral language (DOL) with prepositional practice, consider discipline-related sentences, such as the following:

- Social Studies: The colonists were successful *despite* the adversities they faced *with* inclement weather.
- Math: The numerator is placed *over* a denominator.
- Science: The flower grew *since* the soil was fertilized.

Semantics: Word Meanings

Semantics instruction can tap the vocabulary encountered across all disciplines and genres. If a student has difficulties with semantics—word meanings or vocabulary—then prepare categories to help sort words, along with instruction on synonyms (words with the same meaning), antonyms (words with the opposite meaning), and word origins. At the elementary level, think about words that are associated with categories of money, seasons, living things, planets, measurement, or math operations. At the secondary level, sort words into categories that define and denote relationships. This could involve ancient civilizations, types of organs, or reference tools. For example, neutrons, protons, and electrons are all subatomic materials, but they differ in their charges.

Ask the student to paraphrase his or her understanding of a verbal assignment or highlight key words in a written assignment, with repeated practice to play with words. Explore how although one word may convey a meaning, another word may be even better—it may be more explicit or descriptive for the context. These simple Jack and Jill sentences model a way for very young students to explore vocabulary:

Jack and Jill *went* up the hill.

Jack and Jill *galloped* up the hill.

Jack and Jill *raced* up the hill.

Jack and Jill *charged* up the hill.

Jack and Jill *dashed* up the hill.

Jack and Jill *hurdled* up the hill.

Vocabulary exploration can be further expanded in student writing in all classes—whether it's with a paragraph describing colonial events in U.S. history or explaining the process of meiosis. WordHippo (www.wordhippo.com) is an online tool to explore semantics, including synonyms, antonyms, and rhyming words.

Pragmatics: Language in Social Situations

If a student has difficulties with pragmatics—using oral language, facial expressions, and gestures in conversation and social interactions—then offer instruction and private reminders on listening skills, turn taking, appropriate expression, eye contact, body language, tone of voice, and proximity. Explore ideas at the following sites:

- **ASHA**: www.asha.org/public/speech/development/ PragmaticLanguageTips
- **Do2Learn**: http://do2learn.com/disabilities/CharacteristicsAndStrategies/ SpeechLanguageImpairment_Characteristics.html
- **Understood.org**: www.understood.org/en/learning-attention-issues/ getting-started/what-you-need-to-know/the-difference-between-speech-language-disorders-and-attention-issues
- **Super Duper**: www.superduperinc.com/Handouts/Handout.aspx

Capitalize on every classroom moment to increase the comprehension of everyday functional communications—saying *please* and *thank you;* role playing in skits and plays (see, for example, www.dramanotebook.com/plays-for-kids); giving a weather report; sharing a fashion, movie, or book review; or commenting on a school, community, political, or world event. Students with more intensive speech needs may require social scripts and more repeated practice, along with additional staff and peer supports.

❍ Accompany Written and Verbal Communication with Visuals

Incorporate curriculum pictures and classroom objects with verbal and non-verbal language. Just like students with other differences, students with differing speech-language levels appreciate when visuals and graphic organizers accompany written words. Visuals reinforce the text and illustrate vocabulary that may otherwise be unfamiliar. If discussing the word *column*, for example, the visual depictions in Figure 6.3 better solidify its multiple meanings.

Figure 6.3 | Visual Representations of Columns

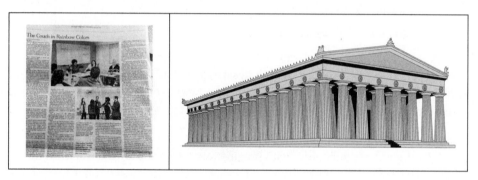

In addition, curriculum organizers are effective ways to present new vocabulary words and ease their understanding. Figures 6.4 and 6.5 are examples for terms that describe the circulatory system and the early European colonies in North America, respectively.

Resources for visuals and graphic organizers across the curriculum include the following:

- **Dipity**: www.dipity.com
- **Freeology**: http://freeology.com/graphicorgs
- **Illustrated Mathematics Dictionary**: www.mathsisfun.com/definitions
- **Inspiration**: www.inspiration.com
- **Merriam-Webster**: www.visualdictionaryonline.com
- **Outline Maps**: www.eduplace.com/ss/maps
- **Pics4Learning**: www.pics4learning.com
- **Read-Write-Think**: www.readwritethink.org/classroom-resources/student-interactives/timeline-30007.html
- **SunCastle Technology**: www.suncastletech.com
- **Visual Science**: http://visual-science.com

Figure 6.4 | Graphic Organizer for Circulation System Vocabulary

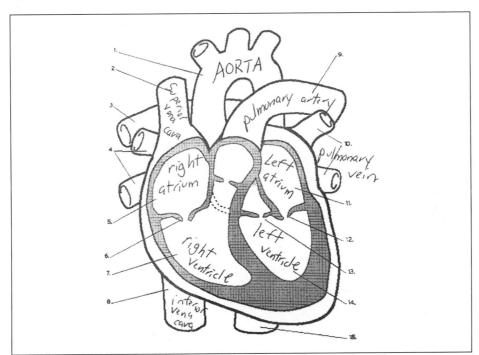

⊙ Explore Assistive Options

Speech is augmented by gestures, body language, and visual expressions. Learn to select, apply, and use assistive technology as needed, such as how to effectively operate augmentative or alternative forms of communication (AAC) to help learners with more severe speech and language disorders. This approach includes, but is not limited to, signing, vocalizations, and symbols on communication boards. It also includes low- and high-tech devices, which range from personalized conversation books to devices programmed to generate speech and conversation. AACs are generally used when speech is nonexistent or considerably limited.

Some students need to hear appropriate fluency modeled by listening either to a teacher or to a recorded example. Monitor and increase students' levels of attentiveness to their own alertness and responses during class discussions. Students can tally the total number of appropriate communications in a class discussion or cooperative peer assignments. They can also view and listen to a video or digital recording of their own language or watch their mouths make speech sounds in a mirror.

Figure 6.5 | Graphic Organizer for Vocabulary Related to Early European Colonies in North America

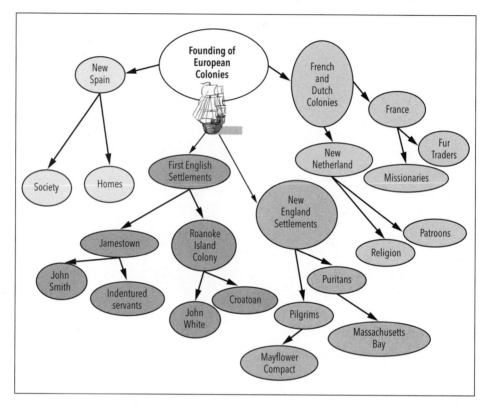

Although learners benefit from technology that synthesizes, recognizes, verifies, and supplies speech—with its diverse curriculum applications—it is important to remember that each device should be selected depending on an individual student's needs. Keep in mind that technology is a tool that must be monitored to ensure that it does not replace creative engagements and meaningful interactions with peers and adults (Jackson, 2015).

Collaborate with All

As noted earlier, it's important to collaborate with the school's SLP in order to monitor student progress with class participation and the application of interventions in the classroom. Often, SLPs offer services and instruction within the classroom during instruction; however, the students with whom they are working should never be singled out. Instead, they should be supported and involved in the same assignments as their peers as much as possible. Research indicates that this collaborative model is more effective than either a classroom-based model that excludes the input of an SLP or a traditional pull-out model for teaching curricular vocabulary to students who receive speech or language services (Throneburg, Calvert, Sturm, Paramboukas, & Paul, 2000). This finding makes the general education classroom a fertile ground for speech services, since its naturalistic and inclusive setting offers vocabulary in context, with classroom peers present. Both academic and social language can improve with increased applications and generalizations. Working in the general education classroom also affords SLPs the opportunity to see and hear students' real language, which then drives the intervention.

Collaboration most certainly includes students' families, with conferences and communication on speech-language levels, strategies, progress, and plans to move forward. Classroom instructional assistants, specialists, and coteachers also need to know each student's speech-language profile. Collaboration encompasses a definition of roles, a belief in parity, and a fidelity to the interventions that honor students' academic levels.

In summary, it is important that speech-language instruction values the following elements discussed in this chapter:

- Individual learner communication profiles
- Determination of student levels
  + Social
  + Academic
  + Communicative
  + Physical
- Appropriate supports for
  + Receptive language
  + Expressive language
  + Phonology
  + Morphology
  + Syntax
  + Semantics
  + Pragmatics
- Ongoing monitoring
- Accompanying visuals
- Functional communication
- Appropriate technologies
- Collaboration

References

American Speech-Language-Hearing Association (ASHA). (2016). Speech, and language disorders and diseases. Available: www.asha.org/public/speech/disorders

Bruce, S. (2010). Introduction to the holistic communication profile: Integrating pivotal social and cognitive milestones in communication programming, Boston College. Available: http://documents.nationaldb.org/Holcommprofile.pdf

Jackson, S. (2015). *Disconnect the tech! Help your child plug into good communication.* Handy Handouts Number 408. Greenville, SC: Super Duper Publications.

Stuttering Foundation. (2016). Stuttering and the king's speech. Available: www.stutteringhelp.org/stuttering-and-kings-speech

Temple University, College of Education, Institute on Disabilities. (2016). www.temple.edu/instituteondisabilities

Throneburg, R., Calvert, L., Sturm, J., Paramboukas A., & Paul, P. (2000). A comparison of service delivery models: Effects on curricular vocabulary skills in the school setting. *American Journal of Speech-Language Pathology, 9,* 10–20.

U.S. National Library of Medicine. (2014). Speech disorders—children. MedlinePlus. Available: www.nlm.nih.gov/medlineplus/ency/article/001430.htm

Professional Resources

American Speech-Language-Hearing Association (ASHA). (2004). Preferred practice patterns for the profession of speech-language pathology. Available: www.asha.org/policy/PP2004-00191

American Speech-Language-Hearing Association (ASHA). (2008). Knowledge and skills needed by speech-language pathologists providing clinical supervision. Available: www.asha.org/policy/KS2008-00294

American Speech-Language-Hearing Association (ASHA). (2016). Roles and responsibilities of speech-language pathologists in schools. Available: www.asha.org/policy/PI2010-00317

Apraxia-Kids. (2013). A comparison of childhood apraxia of speech, dysarthria, and severe phonological disorder. Available: www.apraxia-kids.org/library/a-comparison-of-childhood-apraxia-of-speech-dysarthria-and-severe-phonological-disorder

Blosser, J., Roth, F. P., Paul, D. R., Ehren, B. J., Nelson, N. W., & Sturm, J. M. (2012, August 28). Integrating the core. *The ASHA Leader.*

Informal Phonics Inventory, University of Virginia. Available: www.google.com/search?client=safari&rls=en&q=informal+phonic+inventory&ie=UTF-8&oe=UTF-8

Mayer Johnson: www.mayer-johnson.com

Mayo Clinic. Dysarthria. (2016). www.mayoclinic.org/diseases-conditions/dysarthria/basics/definition/con-20035008

PACE: www.asha.org/uploadedFiles/SLPs-Performance-Assessment-Contributions-Effectiveness.pdf

Teaching Tolerance: www.tolerance.org

7

Students with Auditory Processing Disorder (APD)

The Possible Whys

Research offers mixed opinions about the causes of auditory processing disorder (APD)—often referred to as central auditory processing disorder (CAPD). There is typically no hearing loss with APD, but learners have difficulty processing and interpreting auditory input. The debate exists between theories that indicate impairment in the brain's corpus callosum and executive function deficits (DeBonis, 2015; Hugdahl, 2003; Jerger, 2007). The left hemisphere of the brain, which plays a role in processing language, and the corpus callosum, which assists with communication between the brain's two hemispheres, may be underdeveloped. A right-ear advantage is sometimes found in young children with corpus callosum impairment (Jerger, 2007). There are also links to recurring middle ear infections, head injury, or trauma (Auditory Processing Disorder Foundation, 2012).

The processing of auditory information is complex, with simultaneous engagement of auditory, cognitive, and language mechanisms (Medwetsky, 2011). APD has been attributed as primarily an auditory disorder, but it has also been related to poor working memory. Underlying problems in language comprehension and metalinguistic awareness with listening deficits could be attributable to any number of factors and not be indicative of APD, which often produces an incorrect diagnosis (DeBonis, 2015; Medwetsky, 2011; Ronnberg & Lunner, 2011).

Characteristics and Strengths

According to the National Coalition of Auditory Processing (Lucker, 2016), the signs of APD begin in preschool and continue to manifest throughout adolescence. Students with APD often have trouble understanding speech in noisy environments.

This difficulty affects their ability to follow directions, discriminate tone frequencies, remember what was said in the correct order, and extract and interpret information amid many sounds (American Speech-Language-Hearing Association, 2005). Working memory—which holds, processes, manipulates, and applies information—is weaker.

The issue for a student with APD is not with understanding the meaning of what is said but with hearing the correct message. For example, the oral direction "Open your textbook to page 59; you have 10 minutes to complete the activity" may be heard as "Open your textbook to page 59 in 10 minutes." Although the misinterpretation is close to the original message, the subtle differences heard negatively affect understanding and classroom performance.

Classroom Implications

Auditory processing deficits, especially if background noises are present, affect students' ability to remember details of text when reading, follow classroom rules, apply the rules of a game or sport, recall math facts, apply information learned when taking a test, and perform functional skills such as remembering to eat lunch. Students with APD may also have difficulty enacting class procedures and carrying on conversations.

When written words with unfamiliar vocabulary are verbally delivered, or nonlinguistic supports such as gestures and facial cues are missing, then the processing is even more difficult. Some learners have difficulty processing words spoken by others and have comorbidity of a specific learning disability. Related literacy skills (e.g., phonemic segmentation), learning another language, and applying concepts when the curriculum spirals from grade to grade or even from class to class presents difficulties. Remembering science lab procedures or multistep directions, such as listening to math instruction and then relating several operations to solve a problem, is often challenging. As for all students with differences, strengths may exist in other modalities (e.g., visual, kinesthetic, etc.).

Inclusion Strategies

❯ Tweak the Environment and Maximize the Tools

Consider environmental factors with both low- and high-tech options. This includes placing tennis balls or Velcro on the bottom of chairs to reduce ambient noises or allowing a learner to use headphones to listen to oral directions digitally recorded. Consider the benefits of sound field amplification systems, and allow learners to digitally record class instruction, which students can then play back and repeat at their own pace. Eliminate extra noises whenever possible, such as not seating a student by an open door or window.

❯ Be Patient and Validate

Students with APD value patience, which is particularly important when a student has difficulty rhyming words or developing vocabulary, misreads situations or words, is challenged by verbal instruction, or cannot find the right word in a conversation. Each learner requires patience and validation to strengthen his or her weaknesses. Having patience means that adults and peers face the learner when speaking and maintain eye contact. Rephrase as necessary and ask the student to paraphrase what he or she heard. Remember to validate that APD is not a feigned disorder, nor is it a label for a person who is simply not paying attention.

❯ Provide Experiential Activities with Multimodal Presentations

Think of ways to accompany auditory instruction with additional visuals and experiential activities. If auditory processing skills are weaker, determine preferred learner styles that may be stronger (e.g., kinesthetic, visual). Examples include being certain that students understand the illustrations that accompany a book or providing illustrations if a text has no visuals. Provide appropriate pictures, illustrations, maps, and other visual organizers.

This strategy can be used at any level and with almost any type of text. For example, if an upper elementary or middle school class is reading Jack London's *The Call of the Wild,* provide a map of the Yukon Territory; if reading Christopher Paul Curtis's *Bud, Not Buddy,* share photos taken during the Great Depression. Offer access to a visual or rhyming dictionary in a poetry unit. Activate closed captioning when watching curriculum videos such as those from Khan Academy or BrainPop. Scaffold the multimodal presentations by replaying parts of a presentation or stopping a video to check and reinforce understanding.

Physically demonstrate text, such as incorporating skits to enhance *The Cat in the Hat* on an elementary level or *Hamlet* on a secondary level, instead of only reading the text aloud. Think about how to act out concepts, whether instruction is on the Spanish conquest of the Aztecs or on Newton's Laws of Motion.

The following curriculum example using Shakespeare's *Twelfth Night* illustrates how to support a lesson that bolsters language, memory, attention, and retention skills for students with APD.

1. Present the key events from each of the five acts on index cards that students can reference to remember the play's characters and sequence of events.

2. Offer a Quizlet (with the text-to-speech function activated) that allows students to review the vocabulary and characters with flashcards, games, and digitally created tests.

3. Present the information with novelty, such as the tabloid version produced by the BBC. (www.bbc.co.uk/drama/shakespeare/60secondshakespeare/themes_twelfthnight.shtml)

4. Ask students to create storyboards with hand-drawn pictures and captions of character dialogue. Explore the Read, Write, Think site of the National Council of Teachers of English to create a digital version. (www.readwritethink.org/classroom-resources/student-interactives/comic-creator-30021.html)

In summary, as an advocate for students with APD, it's important to remember to frequently

- Tweak the environment to maximize tools.
- Be patient and validate.
- Provide experiential activities.
- Support, scaffold, and monitor understandings.
- Coordinate and gain information and strategies from speech-language pathologists, audiologists and other service providers who have specialized skills with diagnosis and remediation.
- Be aware of comorbidity factors to respect and honor the needs of a learner who has APD as well as ADHD or another specific learning disability.
- Focus on ways to strengthen the auditory weaknesses with high-interest and diverse classroom presentations.

References

American Speech-Language-Hearing Association. (2005). Central auditory processing disorders. Available: www.asha.org/policy

Auditory Processing Disorder Foundation. (2012). What is auditory processing disorder? Available: www.theapdfoundation.org

DeBonis, D. (2015). It is time to rethink central auditory processing disorder protocols for school-aged children. *American Journal of Audiology, 24*(2), 124–136.

Hugdahl, K. (2003). Dichotic listening in the study of auditory laterality. In K. Hugdahl & R. J. Davidson (Eds.), *The asymmetrical brain*. Cambridge, MA: MIT Press.

Jerger, J. (2007). Editorial: Dichotic listening in the evaluation of APD. *Journal of the American Academy of Audiology, 18*(1), 4.

Lucker, J. (2016). What is APD? National Coalition of Auditory Processing. Available: www.ncapd.org/What_is_APD_.html

Medwetsky, L. (2011). Spoken language processing model: Bridging auditory and language processing to guide assessment and intervention. *Language, Speech, and Hearing Services in Schools, 42*(3), 286–296.

Ronnberg, R., & Lunner, T. (2011). Working memory supports listening in noise for persons with hearing impairment. *Journal of American Academy of Audiology, 22*(3), 156–167.

Professional Resources

American Academy of Audiology. (2010). *Clinical practice guidelines: Diagnosis, treatment, and management of children and adults with central auditory processing disorder.* Reston, VA: Author.

American Speech-Language Hearing Association. (2005). Central auditory processing disorders. Retrieved from Bellis, T. (2002). *When the brain can't hear: Unraveling the mystery of auditory processing disorder.* New York: Atria Books.

Loo, J. H. Y., Bamiou, D. E., & Rosen, S. (2013). The impacts of language background and language-related disorders in auditory processing assessment. *Journal of Speech, Language, and Hearing Research, 56*(1), 1–12.

Understood.org. (2016). Understanding auditory processing disorders. Available: www.understood.org/en/learning-attention-issues/child-learning-disabilities/auditory-processing-disorder/understanding-auditory-processing-disorder

Wallach, G. (2011). Peeling the onion of auditory processing disorder: A language curricular-based perspective. *Language Speech and Hearing Services in Schools, 42*(3), 273–285.

8

Students with Autism Spectrum Disorder (ASD)

The Possible Whys

Students with autism spectrum disorder (ASD) have differences in how various parts of their brain work together, which is attributable to a number of factors. Etiology is attributable to heredity, genetics, and neurological disorders, with differences indicated in brain scans (Autism Society, 2016). Autism studies link ASD to families (Meade-Kelly, 2013), whereas current research is also investigating medical and environmental factors (DeWeerdt, 2015; Mayo Clinic Staff, 2014). Claims have been made that vaccines play a role, but research has found no connection (Centers for Disease Control and Prevention, 2015; Institute of Medicine, 2004). Not vaccinating a child can result in other diseases that could result in serious harm with a spread of viruses and bacteria (Public Health, 2016).

Characteristics and Strengths

The *Diagnostic and Statistical Manual* (DSM-5) of the American Psychiatric Association (2013) includes a single umbrella category of ASD that affects

- Communication and social skills
- Repetitive and stereotyped behaviors

Characteristics range from mild to severe, with onset in early childhood and an effect on a person's level of functioning. ASD and intellectual disabilities often occur together; however, a diagnosis of ASD is not better explained by a global development delay or intellectual disability—with lower levels of social communications and interactions evidenced. Levels of intelligence can range from above to below average, but levels of adaptive behavior are usually lower (Charman et al., 2011).

Students with ASD have lower social communication skills that are persistent and show up across multiple contexts, involving social reciprocity, adjustment to different environments, and the ability to follow structures and routines. Social and emotional differences range from varying levels of imaginative play to a lack of interest in peers. Stereotyped (i.e., repetitive and ritualistic) behaviors—such as lining up toys, twirling, repeating words (echolalia), and preferring sameness—are often evidenced.

Attention, conversation, and reactions to stimuli are often atypical when compared to their age-level peers. Pragmatics, referring here to language or conversation between a speaker and a listener, and social communications are affected. A student with ASD often exhibits communication that is restricted to his or her interests, and verbal behaviors may seem scripted, with a student reciting preferred phrases (e.g., movie dialogue, TV commercials). At times, a student with ASD will not pick up the appropriate cues from his or her environment and have difficulty extracting stimuli or understanding the "hidden curriculum" represented by facial expressions, personal space, eye contact, and other nonverbal actions. Students with ASD also experience seizures, levels of anxiety and depression, and negativity (Frye, 2012; Ozsivadjian, Hibberd, & Hollocks, 2014). Adults with ASD have associated psychological differences that include depression, anxiety, and obsessive-compulsive disorder (Croen et al., 2015).

Sensory processing differences are often evidenced. Hyposensitivity (underresponsiveness to stimuli) is exhibited if a student, for example, feels a need to touch different textures or does not react appropriately to pain. Hypersensitivity (overreaction to stimuli) is exemplified by a student who reacts negatively to the loud ringing of a fire drill bell, is afraid of crowds, or experiences discomfort or anxiety when hugged unexpectedly. Synesthesia (involuntary mingling of senses) can also show up in a student with ASD; examples include seeing colors when looking at letters or hearing music. Some students with autism thus prefer visuals and have an affinity for pictures. Temple Grandin, a professor with autism, describes this phenomenon in her book *Thinking in Pictures*: "I THINK IN PICTURES. Words are like a second language. . . . I translate both spoken and written words into full-color movies, complete with sound, which run like a VCR tape in my head. When somebody speaks to me, his words are instantly translated into pictures" (Grandin, 1995, p.19). In Grandin's initial presentations, she also spoke with her back to the audience, not understanding the implication of eye contact or speaker protocols.

I had the good fortune to meet Kim Peek, whose life is the basis for the character portrayed by Dustin Hoffman in the movie *Rain Man*. His father shared that his son was unable to speak to large groups of people until he held the Academy Award that the film's director, Barry Levinson, gave to him—which then became his talking stick. Peek had an excellent memory, exhibiting savant syndrome, which allowed him to identify the day of the week for any given date and to recall facts related to an event without referencing any text.

Psychological theories of autism outline characteristics attributable to a delayed theory of mind, weak central coherence, and impaired executive function (Constable, Grossi, Moniz, & Ryan, 2013). *Theory of mind* refers to an understanding of other people's points of view or perspectives without strict adherence to one's own perceptions. This includes being aware of how one's actions and behaviors affect others in both positive and negative ways. Students with ASD may experience anxiety, frustration, indifference, and avoidance if other people's choices and actions differ from their personal likes, dislikes, focuses, and demeanors. Central coherence involves having the ability to see the big picture—beyond a fixation on the details. If a student with autism has impaired executive functioning, then he or she has lower organizational and planning skills.

Classroom Implications

Overall, as with other differences, there is no typical autism template. It is a spectrum disorder, with a veritable rainbow of abilities and individualized strengths, and students can display characteristics that range from mild to severe. Thus, the classroom implications are just as diverse.

First and foremost, educate the student with autism and his or her peers about the diverse characteristics that may surface, with a view that highlights the student—not his or her ASD label. Knowledge is essential to increase understanding. Although you never want to single out a student with autism as being "out of the norm," it is a disservice not to encourage peers to embrace certain differences as an asset and to see that a student with autism is not defined by his or her disability but is still a "regular kid" who just happens to see things differently or sometimes behave or react to the environment in a way that another learner might not. The point is to share a view of autism as a difference and not a disorder—which decreases the social barriers learners with ASD often face in inclusionary settings (Owren, 2013). A positive view on difference, whether it references ability, race, language, culture, or sensory realities, requires increased and accurate knowledge and more inclusionary experiences. Overall, the social exclusion of students with ASD needs to be improved with increased empathy and attitudinal changes (Mavropoulou & Sideridis, 2014). Realize that student actions and behaviors, although different or atypical, are not intended to offend. Replace negativity with verbal redirection that helps students with and without ASD increase their metacognition, self-regulation, self-advocacy, empathy, and positive views. Most important, acknowledge the differences as just that—not deficiencies.

Capitalize on student interests to maximize each learner's potential with academic and functional performances in school and life. If a learner with autism is focused on only his or her interests, then navigation of school expectations, rules, and structures is comparable to a labyrinth. This applies to many contexts, not just the classroom—in the school cafeteria and during extracurricular activities, on the bus ride to and from school, during assemblies, and more.

Depending on the student's level of cognitive, social, emotional, behavioral, and communicative impact, literacy, mathematics, language, and oral and written communication can be affected. Cooperative group assignments and class discussion may require differentiated supports and adaptations (e.g., augmentative devices, hand gestures, writing frames, lists of transitional words, increased visuals, more modeling of how to offer eye contact, explanation of how to persevere on an assigned task). Since ASD exists on a spectrum of levels, the interventions should be individualized and never generic.

Literacy is also affected. As an example, when a student who has a lack of central coherence (ability to see the big picture) and loves dogs is reading a story that includes a character with a dog, he or she may concentrate on this minor detail and miss the gist of the whole story, paying little attention to the actions of the main character or plot. A learner with autism thus may lose focus on the central theme, which then spirals to a lack of comprehension. If executive function is affected, then offer additional scaffolding to begin, plan, organize, and complete a set of class expectations and written requirements.

Concentration on sensory details has both positive and negative implications. If a student with autism directs his or her attention on extraneous details, then a walk down the school hallway within a given time frame can be a complicated affair. However, if he or she is on a nature walk, then that attention to details is advantageous. Staff members who know their learners' likes, dislikes, and triggers observe and conference with their students, and they speak with families and other staff to coordinate interventions. Related services include but are not limited to a school- and/or home-based behavioral interventionist, a speech-language pathologist, an occupational and/or physical therapist, and a school counselor.

Inclusion Strategies

❯ Enhance Literacy Instruction with Bibliotherapy

Bibliotherapy uses books to increase mindfulness and an overall awareness of appropriate behavior, as well as to promote self-reflection and positive self-efficacy through textual role models. Experiences can be easier to digest vicariously through fictional characters, rather than learners facing the rules or expectations head-on. Under staff direction, a student with autism and other disabilities uses selected readings to gain and hone language, social, and behavioral skills. The lesson is not hammered home with "This is what you should do or say" but rather revealed through plot and character development so that the student can draw his or her own valuable conclusions to subliminally increase positive behaviors. Bibliotherapy should not be viewed as another thing to teach or do but as a complement to reading and writing instruction, with characters that just happen to have a disability.

While reading *Blue Bottle Mystery* by Kathy Hoopmann during a literature group, a 5th grader told me that the book's character with autism should have done things differently. My student, who was on the spectrum and very similar to the main character, would never have otherwise vocalized these sentiments, but he was better able to recognize some of his own behavioral traits in the character's action and dialogue. Today, this student is my Facebook friend, and I am delighted to follow his college successes.

In addition, staff also gain insights into students with autism (or other disabilities) by reading these types of books themselves, rather than exclusively reading journal articles or learning about a disability during a professional development session. The following list is a sample of the many books that offer relevant insights. For fiction and nonfiction texts with insights on additional disabilities, see Appendix D and this Pinterest board: https://www.pinterest.com/tkarten/disability-books-posted-by-toby-karten.

Bibliotherapy Options

Elementary Level
• *My Friend with Autism* by Beverly Bishop
• *Blue Bottle Mystery* by Kathy Hoopmann
• *My Brother Charlie* by Holly Robinson Peete and Ryan Elizabeth Peete
• *Elemental Island* by Kathy Hoopmann
• *Point to Happy* by Afton Fraser and Miriam Smith
• *Since We're Friends: An Autism Picture Book* by Celeste Shally and David Harrington
• *Ian's Walk* by Laurie Lears

<u>Upper Elementary/Secondary Level</u>

• *Al Capone Does My Shirts* by Gennifer Choldenko
• *Rules* by Cynthia Lord
• *The Reason I Jump* by Naoki Higashida
• *Look Me in the Eye* by John Elder Robison
• *House Rules* by Jodi Picoult
• *A Wizard Alone* by Diane Duane

When I was a coteacher who mentored students as peer helpers for a class with multiple disabilities—including students on the spectrum—we read *My Friend with Autism,* a picture book with captioned illustrations. Although the reading level of this book is geared for students age 5 to 9, its message is on a higher level. Those concepts helped prepare peer mentors in 5th grade, who gained insights into ASD and strategies to assist their mentees—who were often not younger in age but in need of more academic, social, language, and behavioral supports. It was a win-win: the peer helpers gained increased sensitivity through a realistic application of good character skills, and the students with autism were more receptive to guidance from people closer to their age group who mimicked adult directives.

❯ Offer Behavioral Supports

A personalized behavior intervention plan (BIP) is implemented if a student exhibits an unacceptable behavior that needs to be replaced, such as excessive rocking, self-injurious behavior, or a total lack of attention. An applied behavior analysis (ABA) therapist helps students, staff, and families with ways to implement a program that focuses on strategies to increase positive and reduce negative behavior. The BIP entails personalization that respects a student's interests, skill levels, and personal preferences.

Acknowledge the presented behaviors and empower students to tap individual interests to improve upon those behaviors as necessary. I once offered a learner with autism a generic chart to monitor his behavior (Figure 8.1). His instructional assistant informed me that the student decided to modify my behavior chart and replace it with one of his own. His artistic strength is well evidenced by the one he created (Figure 8.2). With collaboration from his instructional assistant, he also added increased specificity and consequently exhibited more buy-in.

Figure 8.1 | Teacher-Generated Behavioral Chart

Time	??? 1pt.	OK 2pts.	Better 3pts.	Good 4pts.	WOW ☺ 5pts.
8:20–8:35 Books away, Do Now					
8:35–10:00 Reading					
10:00–11:00 Math					
11:00–11:45 SS					
12:30–12:50 Spelling					
1:40–2:15 Science					
Column totals					

❯ Break Tasks into Discrete Steps

Try to make abstract concepts concrete by breaking them down into pieces. As examples, offer more explanations and visuals to accompany written and spoken idioms and figurative language. Proactively think about the supports and scaffolding learners require—interpreting actions a character takes in a novel, working effectively in cooperative groups, following class routines (especially if a substitute teacher is present), practicing social narratives, and using scripts to rehearse unfamiliar situations.

Social stories or narratives can break a task into steps but also help students navigate novel environmental cues, including classroom demands (e.g., "Turn to your partner to discuss problem 3," "Please turn to page 112") until the school environment becomes more familiar and routine. Social narratives with visual representations can also be used before entering an unfamiliar setting to help a student with autism preview expected behaviors and routines for hypothetical or real upcoming situations. Sensory elements and social expectations are outlined to ease transitions (e.g., "When we visit the library, we will speak in soft whispers"). Social stories replace a stress-filled and unfamiliar place with a rehearsed one that becomes part of a student's prior knowledge.

Figure 8.2 | Student-Modified Behavioral Chart

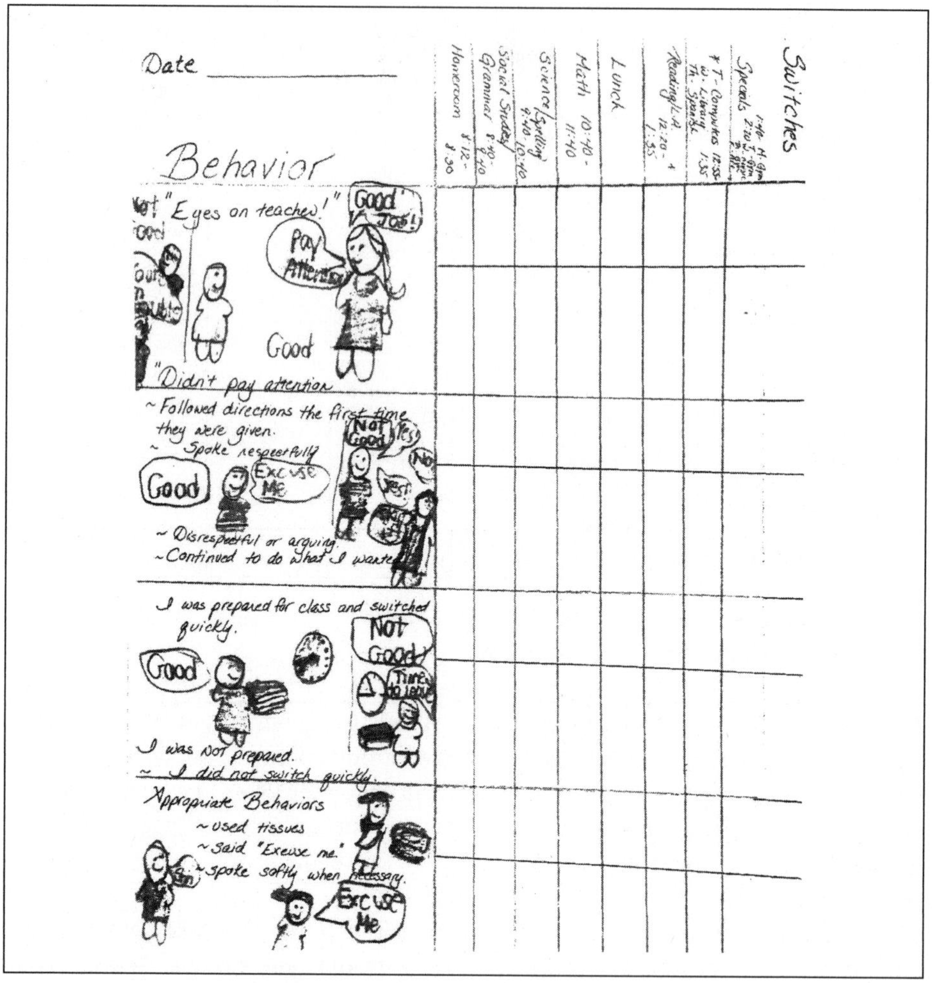

The Theater Development Fund (TDF) offers social narratives for Broadway performances for students with autism, along with other accommodations and modifications. For some shows, there are special autism-friendly performances that have less sensory stimulation through lower visual and auditory input, adjusted lighting, headphones, fidget toys, and other scaffolding that a person with autism may require to appreciate the performance. Figure 8.3 shares part of a social narrative for a Broadway performance that students can review in advance.

Figure 8.3 | Social Narrative for a Broadway Play

An usher will give us a Playbill. A Playbill is a book. I can look at the Playbill.

The theater will get dark and quiet. I will try to be quiet during the show so I can hear everything.

I will see actors wearing costumes on the stage.

More information on making the theater accessible for people with autism, from providing more breaks to dealing with louder noises, is available at Autism Theatre Initiative (www.tdf.org/nyc/40/Autism-Theatre-Initiative). Explore the following resources for additional visuals and organizers:

- **Pics4Learning:** www.pics4learning.com
- **Read, Write, Think:** www.readwritethink.org/files/resources/interactives/trading_cards_2
- **Visual schedules:** https://handsinautism.iupui.edu/pdf/How_To_Visual_Schedules.pdf
- **Affirmation and cue cards:** www.autismspeaks.org/family-services/resource-library/visual-tools
- **Personalized class calendars:** https://developers.google.com/apps-script/reference/calendar/calendar

Capitalize on Student Strengths and Perspectives

Think about naturalistic interventions, meaning those that occur in the context of daily routines. Capitalize on student strengths, which for students with autism often includes heightened visual awareness. Use visual representations, such as comic strips, frequently; employ video modeling to increase awareness of positive behaviors; and use graphic organizers to outline big ideas before students get overly focused on (and distracted by) extraneous details. Think about how to assist, but not enable, students. Say what you mean explicitly, explaining idioms and abstract comments, since students with autism might otherwise take these statements literally. Avoid sarcasm. Be certain to know how students' perspectives relate to their families, needs, and everyday realities—whether that includes interest (or lack thereof) in mathematics, how to transition between classes with additional hallway noises or distractions, reactions to stimuli such as loud music or a stiff shirt or wooly sweater, or reactions to family and school routines and rules. Share resources, tools, and strategies you find helpful with families so they can help reinforce learning; improve retention; and support behavioral, social, and academic demands at home. That might mean having a student use visual cue cards with a family member or an assignment pad to check for homework completion. A student with ASD who needs a staff member to provide increased proximity (to ensure that attention is maximized in school) also requires similar home monitoring to ensure maximum performance.

As with all differences, it's important to offer appropriate levels of feedback and praise. Temple Grandin (2016) offers strategies that value waiting for a student to respond and capitalizing on teachable moments, rather than going full steam ahead with instruction that does not acknowledge how a student with ASD perceives the content, routines, and expectations. Kathy Hoopmann, an author of children's books about autism, views autism as a celebration of differences. One of her characters in *The Blue Bottle* Mystery—Andy, who does not have autism—was envious of his friend Ben who was on the spectrum because math, science, and computers came easier to him. He related to Ben because he was shorter and could not be on the basketball team. These two fictional characters mimic real-life people since they remind us to highlight the strengths inside all of us and not to allow a difference to define a person's capabilities or self-efficacy. Everyone is capable of reaching great heights when high expectations and appropriate scaffolding are the norm.

To sum up, when teaching students with autism, it's important to remember to

- Highlight and empower the student, not the ASD label.
- Teach, not judge.

- Spin weaker communications into productive discussions.
- Offer social skills training.
- Praise positive interactions with peers and adults.
- Leverage peers as mentors.
- Offer behavioral supports to replace repetitive and stereotypic behaviors.
- Enhance literacy instruction with bibliotherapy.
- Value self-regulation.
- Break tasks into discrete steps, including the use of social narratives.
- Accompany the abstract with visual supports.
- Collaborate with related service providers and families.
- Capitalize on student strengths and perspectives.
- Appreciate and honor a different way of seeing the world.

References

American Psychiatric Association. (2013). *Diagnostic and statistical manual of mental disorders: DSM-5* (5th ed.). Washington, DC: Author.

Autism Society. (2016). Causes. Available: www.autism-society.org/what-is/causes

Centers for Disease Control and Prevention. (2015). Vaccines do not cause autism. Available: www.cdc.gov/vaccinesafety/concerns/autism.html

Charman, T., Pickles, A., Simnoff, E., Chandler, S. Loucas, T., & Baird, G. (2011). IQ in children with autism disorders: Data from the Special Needs and Autism Project (SNAP) *Psychological Medicine, 41*(3) 619–627.

Constable, S., Grossi, B., Moniz, A., & Ryan, L. (2013). Meeting the Common Core State Standards for students with autism: The challenge for educators. *Teaching Exceptional Children, 45*(3), 6–13.

Croen, L., Zerbo, O., Qian, Y., Massolo, M., Rich, S., Sidney, S, & Kripke, C. (2015). The health status of adults on the autism spectrum. *International Journal of Research and Practice, 19*(7), 814–823.

DeWeerdt, S. (2015). What environmental factors cause autism? Available: www.slate.com/articles/health_and_science/medical_examiner/2015/11/what_causes_autism_environmental_risks_are_hard_to_identify.html

Frye, R. (2012). Seizures in autism spectrum disorder. *Talk About Curing Autism* (TACA). Available: www.tacanow.org/family-resources/seizures

Grandin, T. (1995). *Thinking in pictures and other reports from my life with autism*. New York: Vintage Books.

Institute of Medicine. (2004). *Immunization safety review. Vaccines and autism board of health promotion and disease prevention*. Washington, DC: National Academy Press.

Mavropoulou, S., & Sideridis, G. (2014). Knowledge of autism and attitudes of children towards their partially integrated peers with autism spectrum disorders. *Journal of Autism and Developmental Disorders, 44*(8), 1867–1885.

Mayo Clinic Staff. (2014). Autism spectrum disorder: Risk factors. Available: www.mayoclinic.org/diseases-conditions/autism-spectrum-disorder/basics/risk-factors/con-20021148

Meade-Kelly, V. (2013). New research investigates inherited causes of autism. *Broad Institute.* www.broadinstitute.org/news/4624

Owren, T. (2013). Neurodiversity: Accepting autistic difference. *Learning Disability Practice, 16*(4), 32–37.

Ozsivadjian, A., Hibberd, C., & Hollocks, M. (2014). Brief report: The use of self-report measures in young people with autism spectrum disorder to access symptoms of anxiety, depression and negative thoughts. *Journal of Autism and Developmental Disorders, 4*(44), 969–974.

Public Health. (2016). Understanding vaccines: Vaccine myths debunked. Available: www.publichealth.org/public-awareness/understanding-vaccines/vaccine-myths-debunked

---

Professional Resources

Autism NOW Center and the Autistic Self-Advocacy Network. (2014). Welcome to the autistic community. Available: http://autisticadvocacy.org/wp-content/uploads/2014/02/WTTAC-Adolescent-FINAL-2.pdf

ASD Pinterest: www.pinterest.com/tkarten/asd-adjust-strategies-dynamically

Autism Speaks. (2016). Applied behavior analysis. Available: www.autismspeaks.org/what-autism/treatment/applied-behavior-analysis-aba

Autism Speaks. Visual tools. Available: www.autismspeaks.org/family-services/resource-library/visual-tools

Ayres, K., Mechling, L., & Sansosti, F. J. (2013). The use of mobile technologies to assist with life skills/dependence of students with moderate/severe intellectual disability and/or autism spectrum disorders: Considerations for the future of school psychology. *Psychology in the Schools, 50*(3), 259–271.

Battaglia, A. A., & Radley, K. C. (2014). Peer-mediated social skills training for children with autism spectrum disorder. *Beyond Behavior, 23*(2), 4–13.

Brain Balance Achievement Centers (2016). Signs and symptoms of sensory processing disorder. Available: www.brainbalancecenters.com/blog/2012/04/signs-and-symptoms-of-sensory-processing-disorder

Centers for Disease Control and Prevention. Autism spectrum disorder (ASD). (2013). Available: www.cdc.gov/ncbddd/autism/hcp-dsm.html

Do2Learn. (2016). Autism spectrum disorder. Available: http://do2learn.com/disabilities/CharacteristicsAndStrategies/AutismSpectrumDisorder_Strategies.html

Hallahan, D., Kauffman, J., & Pullen, P. (2015). *Exceptional learners: An introduction to special education* (13th ed.). Boston: Pearson/Allyn & Bacon.

Hoopmann, K. (2001). *Blue bottle mystery: An Asperger adventure.* London: Jessica Kingsley.

National Professional Development Center on Autism Spectrum Disorders: www.autismpdc.fpg.unc.edu

Neitzel, J., Boyd, B., Odom, S. L., & Edmondson Pretzel, R. (2008). *Peer-mediated instruction and intervention for children and youth with autism spectrum disorders: Online training module.* Chapel Hill: University of North Carolina, National Professional Development Center on Autism Spectrum Disorders, FPG Child Development Institute. Available: www.autisminternetmodules.org

Temple Grandin website: www.templegrandin.com/templegrandinart.html

9
Students with Intellectual Disabilities (ID)

The Possible Whys

An intellectual disability (ID) has diverse causes, including genetic factors, difficulties experienced during pregnancy or delivery, and environmental health hazards. Impairments to brain development before or during birth can result from temporary oxygen deprivation; other birth injuries; childhood diseases that lead to brain injury, such as meningitis and encephalitis; congenital hyperthyroidism; inadequate health care; lead, mercury, and environmental toxins; chromosomal disorders; a pregnant mother's use of alcohol or drugs; or malnutrition. The three main causes of intellectual disability, however, are Down syndrome, fetal alcohol syndrome, and fragile X syndrome (The Arc, 2011).

Characteristics and Strengths

Although the majority of children with Down syndrome have mild to moderate intellectual disability (Arc, 2016), similar to students with autism and other disabilities that exist on a "spectrum," the characteristics and severity vary. A scene in Kim Edwards's book *The Memory Keeper's Daughter* offers a view of a student with Down syndrome through a strength paradigm. Two of Edwards's characters—who have children with Down syndrome—ponder, "What would happen, they conjectured, if they simply went on assuming their children would do *everything*. Perhaps not quickly. Perhaps not by the book. But what if they simply erased those growth and development charts, with their precise, constricting points and curves? What if they kept their expectations but erased the time line? What harm could it do? Why not try?" (Edwards, 2005, p. 98).

The point here is to view students with ID as individual learners who achieve successes on their own timetable. Deviation from so-called typical peers does not need to translate to deficiency.

An intellectual disability is a developmental disability, occurring before the age of 18, that affects intellectual functioning and adaptive behavior. *Intellectual functioning* refers to one's general mental capacity, such as learning, reasoning, and problem solving (American Association of Intellectual and Developmental Disabilities [AAIDD], 2013). *Adaptive behavior* includes the application of practical, conceptual, and social skills, which are basically referred to as a category of functional life skills to navigate daily activities in school and the larger community. Practical life skills include activities of daily living (personal care), including those that relate to occupational skills; health care; nutrition; travel/transportation; schedules/routines; safety; the use of money, cell phones, and calendars; and so forth. Conceptual skills involve abstract thinking, such as the generalization and transfer of concepts, reasoning, and problem solving in both academic and social domains. Conceptual areas also influence skills with listening, speaking, reading, writing, mathematics, memory, general knowledge, and critical reasoning. Social skills entail adult and peer interactions, along with establishing and maintaining interpersonal relationships and friendships and communicating effectively (American Psychiatric Association [APA], 2013).

In the past, standardized tests that ostensibly measured intelligence quotient (IQ) were the main way to diagnose intellectual disabilities. IQ tests are still used today, but clinical assessments across the conceptual, social, and practical domains also offer important information. This includes how a learner is functioning and the appropriate interventions that are necessitated, based on everyday application of skills learned, rather than on a fixed notion that caps a student's potential. Linguistic and cultural diversity is also vital to consider, since these differences affect a student's learning rate. AAIDD notes that one is never to assume that strengths do not exist, despite evidenced limitations. They also emphasize that when linguistic and cultural difference are considered, racism and cultural bias cannot enter the ID diagnosis (Goode, 2015). Comorbidity is possible, since some students with ID also have, for example, dyslexia, attention deficit hyperactivity disorder, or autism spectrum disorder (APA, 2015; also see Chapters 1, 2, and 8, respectively, on these disabilities).

Classroom Implications

Students with ID learn but in different ways. For example, they typically benefit from concrete presentations, step-by-step approaches, and additional repetition, practice, and modeling to achieve fluency and generalizations. As warranted, assistance with social interactions, communication, self-help, and adaptive daily living skills may be required through personalized visual schedules; mobile devices (such as an iPad) to communicate with a symbol-based app that offers alternative and augmentative communication (AAC); and discrete task analysis of academic, social, and procedural skills. Different levels of school support are offered, with a combination of services in locations specified in the student's individualized education program (IEP). Placements and services are individually determined and customized based on learner profiles. Thus, a student with ID may be in a self-contained classroom with other students with disabilities, participate in an inclusive general education classroom for all or part of the day, receive related services such as occupational and physical therapy or speech-language services, partner with an instructional assistant, or have an extended school year.

To summarize the classroom support students with ID require, Canella-Mallone, Konrad, and Pennington (2015) offer the acronym ACCESS:

Accommodations and assistive technologies

Concrete topics

Critical skills

Explicit instruction

Strategy instruction

Systematic evaluation

Inclusion Strategies

➲ Monitor Progress toward Outcomes

Like students with other disabilities, students with intellectual disabilities should have access to the general education curriculum, and their progress should be monitored. The appropriate supports (e.g., peer mentors, increased metacognition, additional prompts and visuals) are placed within the inclusive general education classroom, if it has been determined to be the least restrictive environment by the IEP team (which consists of school staff, families, and all other related service providers). A label of intellectual disability does not imply that a separate classroom is routine practice. Each student with ID is an individual who is entitled to a free and appropriate education alongside his or her peers without disability.

Progress toward reaching IEP goals is reviewed and shared at set intervals and then guides future instructional decisions. Any steps toward increased metacognition and mastery of skills are praised. As an example, if a student compares two sets of objects to determine which set is greater, but he or she has difficulties with one-to-one correspondence, then point out that even though an incorrect answer was obtained, the student did give an answer that was closer than the last attempt. The same holds true for a student who misses only one letter while spelling a word or reads a sentence but leaves out one word. The learning journey has obstacles, but sharing progress along the way and remaining positive help students with intellectual differences gain self-efficacy and make additional strides.

❯ Diversify the Supports

A spectrum of supports exists for learners with ID. This includes learning, communication, and physical supports for both academic and functional skills in the conceptual, social, and practical domains. Read on for more detailed applications in each of these three domains.

Conceptual Domain Scaffoldings

If written expression is difficult and a student cannot organize or formulate an essay, offer the student an outline of the basic facts that need to be edited into cohesive paragraphs, one paragraph at a time. Provide models and additional scaffolding such as concise verbiage, especially if the topic is not within a student's prior knowledge. If a student demonstrates poor fine-motor coordination and weaker physical dexterity or posture, then allow the use of a thicker stylus or a slant board to write so these difficulties do not become obstacles for that student to express his or her understandings and complete written assignments. Offer keyboarding instruction or an accommodation to dictate spelling words into a digital recorder instead of writing responses, if this type of support is needed to demonstrate knowledge.

If a student with intellectual disability is weak in rhyming word patterns and has lower fluency, then instruct him or her in how to use a rhyming and/or electronic speaking dictionary, and use digital tools to read books that honor his or her age level, with high interest but lower reading level. Read 180, High Noon, Perfection, and Steck-Vaughn are some publishers that offer appropriate books for adolescents who read at lower levels. Consider selections by Shel Silverstein, Maya Angelou, or Langston Hughes for instruction with rhyming words, rather than a text such as *Sheep in a Jeep* for a teen with ID.

Conceptual scaffolding in an inclusive setting offers step-by-step assistance with the academic material the class is working on, infused with appropriate supports that provide access for students with ID. The scaffolding allows instruction to be provided on a level that does not frustrate students but explicitly teaches content with concrete models, systematic review, feedback, and reinforcement (Allor, Mathes, Roberts, Jones, & Champlin, 2010). As an example, a modified system of prompts taught learners with moderate intellectual disability to increase their comprehension of 5th-grade U.S. history (Wood, Browder, & Flynn, 2015). Portions of the text were read aloud to students with ID. This oral read was accompanied by instructional strategies on how to answer questions. Learners identified if the answer was or was not in the text and then responded to literal questions. Resources and tools provided included *wh*-graphic organizers—a handout with *who-what-when-why-where* ellipses to sort out facts and details—outlining text headings, and self-monitoring sheets. These types of support allow students with ID to understand and process abstract language and concepts in nonfiction text. Wood and colleagues note that students with ID improved their listening and reading comprehension after these interventions.

Social Domain Scaffoldings

Assistance with adult and peer interactions includes teaching and modeling effective communication and behaviors. Students with intellectual disabilities may show frustration through behaviors that will cause a peer without ID to shy away from him or her or, conversely, to bully the student with ID (Reiter & Lapidot-Lefler, 2007). Bullying is an intolerable situation that requires increased social competencies and behavioral interventions for all students. School policies need to be strictly enforced.

Loneliness and depression may result from isolation and exclusion by age-level peers who learn alongside a peer with intellectual disability but never invite that student to enjoy social activities outside the classroom. Direct instruction on how to develop and maintain friendships—with modeling, social scripts and narratives, and an ongoing conversation—helps all learners. In addition, embedded video and computer-based instruction describe appropriate social skills, showing examples and nonexamples within natural environments (Simpson, Langone, & Ayres, 2004). A computer-based program that contains video clips of peers without disabilities to share examples and nonexamples can be designed to target social skills such as sharing, following directions, and engaging in social greetings. The students are then required to discriminate examples from nonexamples to better identify the appropriate interactions and behaviors in the video and to replicate the behavior (see Figure 9.1).

Abstract social and emotional instruction is not easily qualified or quantified (in contrast to something like a math exam or reading test). However, the same direct step-by-step instruction and progress monitoring are required. Areas of progress to note include inter- and intrapersonal skills such as self-advocacy, personal responsibility, self-esteem, self-efficacy, gullibility, naïveté, peer relationships, and adherence to rules and structure.

Practical Domain Scaffoldings and Task Analysis

Use a diverse approach to improve students' self-regulation and increase their self-efficacy with everyday tasks. Skills in the practical domain include exhibiting personal responsibility and showing increased independence across multiple settings and situations. Schools need to embed practical skills into academic tasks. As examples, involve students as cashiers in classroom or school stores. Students then learn to better organize merchandise, label items, relate to others, and manage money. Infuse literacy and numeracy skills in cooking, gardening, art, and musical projects across the disciplines to consider how academics connect to social, emotional, behavioral, and functional skills.

Task Analysis:

Step 1: I entered the classroom and went to my seat as the teacher took attendance.

Step 2: Next, I took out the homework assignment and shared my answers.

Step 3: I listened to the instruction, followed spoken and written directions, and interacted with my peers.

Step 4: After that, I completed the exit card and handed it to the teacher.

Step 5: Finally, when the bell rang, I gathered the books I needed for my next class.

Figure 9.1 | Discrete Task Analysis Tally Sheet

Days	Step 1	Step 2	Step 3	Step 4	Step 5	Total
Mon						
Tues						
Wed						
Thurs						
Fri						

Academic instruction should include practical literacy about money, time, and number concepts that have ties to a learner's navigation of his or her community, country, and world. If students are learning about Linnaeus's taxonomy and classification system, then a student with intellectual disability may very well receive instruction on more general aspects of classification, such as how food or toiletries are organized in supermarkets and drug stores (in aisles). Functional skills in the practical domain employ text messages, greetings, personal narratives, journal entries, captions for pictures brought in from home, and (as appropriate for age and skill level) résumés and cover letters. It is essential to keep staff, student, and family eyes on transitional skills and establish plans that address academic and functional achievements leading to careers and postsecondary options.

The purpose of school is to guide students on a path to independence to lead productive adult lives. However, students with ID are substantially less likely to participate in postsecondary education when compared to youth with other disabilities (Grigal, 2016). Schools can ease transitions with preparation that involves both academic and social skills, which include ensuring emotional well-being, making choices, navigating online sites, and learning how to dress and act on the job.

❂ Discover and Connect: Be Aware of Prior Knowledge

Personalization is paramount. Always discover and connect to students' strengths, interests, abilities, and prior knowledge. If a student with Down syndrome has lower math counting skills but loves cheerleading, then incorporate counting skills as he or she choreographs dance steps. Determine if a learner knows how to express a ratio as a fraction in its simplest form, before more complex math representations in ratios and proportions invite frustrations. A student who loves a television show or has a favorite movie could learn reading and writing skills centered around it. This could involve summarizing a plot, writing an online critique, or comparing and contrasting movies. However, this same student may need a writing frame to get started or a Venn diagram to help him or her compare and contrast. Strive to get to know your student with ID just as you do all students.

Students relate well to both intrinsic and extrinsic rewards, but those rewards need to be student-specific. One educator related that she offered a student with intellectual disability additional time in physical education class to help the teacher, but it turns out that he preferred helping the librarian instead. The takeaway here is that rewards respond to individual likes and interests. No student is a clone of the next. Students with ID may have weaker expressive skills, but taking the time to know your students increases their motivation. Instruction, feedback, and reinforcement are valuable tools and resources but only if they match students' unique levels and interests.

❂ Share Responsibilities

Share responsibilities among all staff, families, and students. Offer feedback on student progress with families. Establish strong and ongoing home-school communications that allow families to replicate a learning environment and strengthen retention. Provide a structured peer-support system within the class and school by training age-level models and mentors to help students with ID sharpen their academic, social, and communication skills. Often, if a student teaches a concept to a peer, that student strengthens his or her own knowledge as well. Hence, mentoring is a win-win prospect.

When staff share responsibilities, instruction can be offered in smaller parallel groups or centers, dropping the educator-student ratio so students get more focused attention. If a student with intellectual disability is receiving instruction within a cotaught general education class, then the general and special education teachers establish a parity of roles in planning, instruction, and assessment. Paraprofessionals, sometimes called paras or instructional assistants, are often assigned to assist (or "shadow") a student with ID and provide academic and behavioral supports. The conundrum is that not all paraprofessionals receive adequate training to improve educational outcomes for students with ID (Brock & Carter, 2013).

In order to share responsibilities effectively, all staff need to know the facts on an individual student, as well as how to deliver the selected interventions. Again, as with families and students, communication, knowledge, and training are essential for all staff. This means that the music, computer, art, and foreign language teachers, for example, all need to be equally informed of the directives in each student's IEP. There also needs to be ongoing communication between related service providers—such as speech-language pathologists, occupational therapists, and physical therapists—if students with ID are receiving these services.

❂ Learn from Rosa

I once instructed Rosa Marcellino's physical education teacher in a graduate-level course about disabilities and inclusion supports. Rosa, a young girl with Down syndrome, and her family are responsible for Rosa's Law (PL 111-256), which in 2010 replaced the term *mental retardation* with *intellectual disability* in federal laws (Teaching Tolerance, 2011). The educator in my class shared that Rosa and her family's determination sparked him to think differently and teach better. Educating Rosa transformed him into a teacher who was more responsive to learners' possibilities—not their presented or perceived limitations.

The general education classroom is an environment that is an appropriate placement choice as the least restrictive environment if the specially designed supports are in place to meet a learner's unique levels and needs. Overall, teachers should provide accommodations that do not dilute learning outcomes. When modifications are necessary, establish a plan to fade support. The key is to challenge, not enable, students. Students should have access to broader horizons and be encouraged to think about possibilities, not limitations.

To sum up, as an advocate for students with intellectual disabilities, it's important to remember to value

- Progress and mastery.
- Conceptual, practical, and social domains.
- Diversified supports and multisensory deliveries.
- Concretization of abstract concepts.
- High expectations.
- Ways to dissect complex tasks into their components.
- Prior knowledge.
- Connections to student interest.
- Transitional skills.
- The "Rosas" you meet.

References

Allor, J., Mathes, P., Roberts, K., Jones, F., & Champlin, T. (2010). Teaching students with moderate intellectual disabilities to read: An experimental examination of a comprehensive reading intervention. *Education and Training in Autism and Developmental Disabilities, 45*(1), 3–22.

American Association of Intellectual and Developmental Disabilities. (2013). Definition of intellectual disability. Available: http://aaidd.org/intellectual-disability/definition#

American Psychiatric Association. (2013). *Diagnostic and Statistical Manual: DSM-5: Intellectual disability fact sheet.* Available: www.dsm5.org/documents/intellectual%20disability%20fact%20sheet.pdf

The Arc. (2011). Causes and prevention. Available: www.thearc.org/what-we-do/resources/fact-sheets/causes-and-prevention

The Arc. (2016). Down syndrome. Available: www.thearc.org/learn-about/down-syndrome

Brock, M., & Carter, E. (2013). A systematic review of paraprofessional-delivered educational practices to improve outcomes for student with intellectual and developmental disabilities. *Research and Practice for Persons with Severe Disabilities, 38*(4), 211–221.

Canella-Mallone, H., Konrad, M., & Pennington, R. (2015). ACCESS! Teaching writing skills to students with intellectual disability. *Teaching Exceptional Children, 47*(5), 272–280.

Edwards, K. (2005). *The memory keeper's daughter.* New York: Viking.

Goode, T. (2015). Cultural diversity and cultural and linguistic competence: Definitions and conceptual frameworks within the contexts of intellectual and developmental disabilities. Available: http://nccc.georgetown.edu/leadership/2015/Pt1%20CLC%20Definitions%20and%20Frameworks%20043015.pdf

Grigal, M. (2016). Comparing state vocational rehabilitation agency support of higher education access for people with intellectual and other disabilities. Available: www.thinkcollege.net/images/stories/FF6_D2.pdf

Reiter, S., & Lapidot-Lefler, N. (2007). Bullying among special education students with intellectual disabilities: Differences in social adjustment and social skills. *Intellectual and Developmental Disabilities, 45*(3), 174–181.

Simpson, A., Lanone, J., & Ayres, K. (2004). Embedded video and computer based instruction to improve social skills for students with autism. *Education and Training in Developmental Disabilities, 39*(3), 240–252.

Teaching Tolerance. (2011). A girl and a word. Available: www.tolerance.org/magazine/number-39-spring-2011/feature/girl-and-word

Wood, L., Browder, D., & Flynn, L. (2015). Teaching students with intellectual disability to use a self-questioning strategy to comprehend social studies text for an inclusive setting. *Research and Practice for Persons with Severe Disabilities, 40*(4), 275–293.

Professional Resources

AssistiveWare, Proloquo2Go: www.assistiveware.com/product/proloquo2go

Center for Parent Information and Resources. (2011). Intellectual disability. Available: www.parentcenterhub.org/repository/intellectual

Do2Learn. (2016). Intellectual disabilities: Strategies. Available: http://do2learn.com/disabilities/CharacteristicsAndStrategies/IntellectualDisability_Strategies.html

Karten, T. (2013). *Inclusion coaching for collaborative schools.* Thousand Oaks, CA: Corwin.

National Down Syndrome Society. (2012). What is Down syndrome? Available: www.ndss.org/Down-Syndrome/What-Is-Down-Syndrome

National Organization on Fetal Alcohol Syndrome: www.nofas.org

Think College! College Options for People with Intellectual Disabilities: www.thinkcollege.net

YAI, Seeing Beyond Disability: www.yai.org

10
Students with Deafness and Hearing Impairments

The Possible Whys

A variety of prenatal and postnatal causes for deafness is possible, including premature birth, head injury, genetics, or health complications during pregnancy. A lack of oxygen and jaundice during pregnancy may lead to ear infections that can cause hearing impairments, as can complications from rubella, measles, meningitis, mumps, and ototoxic drugs that can cause damage to the inner ear (Deaf Child Worldwide, 2016). Other causes include malformation of the outer and middle ear and ear canal, allergies, childhood infection, and perforated eardrums.

Three types of hearing loss are possible: conductive, sensorineural, and mixed. Conductive hearing loss involves the ear canal, eardrum, and/or middle ear, whereas sensorineural loss includes inner ear and nerve-related causes. Mixed hearing loss involves a combination of difficulties with inner, middle, and outer ear (cochlea) or auditory nerve damage (Hearing Loss Association of America, 2016).

Characteristics and Strengths

Deafness is not synonymous with disability or dysfunction (Benedict, n.d.). Although spoken language and speech development are affected by hearing differences, literacy and math skills may still be strengths and intelligence is not inherently lowered. As with all students with disabilities, a range of needs and performance levels is possible, so characteristics and strengths are equally diverse. Not every student who is deaf is a visual learner, nor is every student with hearing impairment the same. Characteristics are related to the age of onset, degree of deafness or hearing loss, the student's family's hearing status, the degree of residual hearing that might exist, and the types of supports and communication choices the student uses. Families and students have preferred ways of communicating, including the following:

- Oral: speech reading, lip reading, and the use of any residual hearing
- Manual: sign language and finger spelling
- Total communication: a combination of oral and manual methods

Some families and their children embrace American Sign Language (ASL) exclusively and some are bilingual, speaking English as well. When students have parents who are also deaf, they often do better with academic and social areas; some researchers attribute this success to the parents' ability to better communicate with their child (Hallahan, Kaufman, & Pullen, 2012).

The Deaf culture is an active one with common bonds. It differs from the medical model of deafness that views deafness as a loss of function or pathology (Benedict, n.d.). Deaf activists, for example, might question a person's use of cochlear implants and genetic engineering, viewing it as a search for a "cure" for deafness, rather than acceptance.

Learners with a hearing impairment often possess stronger visual and haptic modalities and respond better to multimodal presentations that downplay verbal delivery. Even people who have residual hearing may still rely primarily on visual media to assist their learning. Visual-spatial preferences and environments are considered inside and outside the general education classroom. A visual-spatial learner values images, pictures, digital animations, movies, and media that allow words to be seen as images rather than exclusively as symbols. Visual language uses the hands, faces, bodies, and eyes, rather than sound through auditory presentations (Benedict, n.d.).

Classroom Implications

The Commission on Education of the Deaf has outlined recommendations for changes in the way that the federal government supports the education and social development of individuals who are deaf from birth (U.S. Department of Education, 2015). The concern is that their unique communication and language needs are not being met in general education classrooms, because deafness and hearing impairment are a lower-incidence disability, and school staff often have not had prior experiences or appropriate training. If specially designed instruction is not delivered, then the general education classroom becomes a less than optimal site for a free and appropriate public education, as required under the Individuals with Disabilities Education Act (IDEA). Specific concerns include offering instruction for language skills alongside grade level–appropriate reading, writing, spelling, grammar, and mathematical skills—taught in a way that students learn best, which may or may not include oral, manual, and total communication methods.

Students often have difficulties with grammatical complexity and spoken, written, and oral comprehension across the disciplines. They can also be more introspective and experience higher degrees of social isolation if they are not included with their peers in instructional delivery and extracurricular activities. This is the case even though their learning capacities and academic achievements may be comparable to peers without hearing loss or deafness.

Inclusion Strategies

❯ Value Explicit Instruction and Appropriate Scaffolding

As with other differences, inclusion strategies that address hearing impairments should be individualized, based on the student's characteristics. If a student falls behind in reading, language arts, or math, then inclusion strategies should try to strengthen these academic weaknesses with explicit instruction and appropriate scaffolding. Examples include phonics-based reading with increased visuals, hand signals for vowel sounds, tapping out each syllable, written outlines, and more visual organization. Categorizing words into separate columns for definitions and relationships, using mind maps with illustrations that depict concepts, and making other graphic organizers that allow academic vocabulary to be better understood are appreciated. Daily grammar and language instruction for oral and written expression, and more manipulatives and practice for math instruction are essential. Always activate the closed captioning on curriculum videos. Increase the use of manipulatives, which can range from counting chips to raised relief maps, and lessen your reliance on verbal instructions or lectures. The ultimate goal is to avoid letting hearing differences interfere with the development and advancement of academic, critical thinking, and social skills.

❯ Differentiate; Do Not Dilute

Presentations given in the general education classroom should not be diluted—just differentiated. As an example, hand students a copy of a class lecture so they can follow along as you speak or distribute an outline that previews or accompanies the oral instruction to maximize participation and understanding. Cloze notes, in which students fill in missing words or concepts, are also helpful. The cloze notes in Figure 10.1 on the topic of westward expansion offer an example. The word box beneath the notes is optional. If students have difficulty keeping pace, they can choose the appropriate answer from the word box. Nevertheless, keep in mind that the cloze note accommodation does not alter the ultimate outcome of having good student-created notes to reference.

Figure 10.1 | Westward Expansion Cloze Notes

In 1803, President _____ _____ purchased the territory of Louisiana from the _____ government for $15 million. The _____ Purchase stretched from the Mississippi River to the_____ Mountains and from _____ to New Orleans, and it doubled the size of the _____ _____.

| a. westward | c. United States | e. Louisiana | g. Spanish |
| b. Thomas Jefferson | d. Rocky | f. French | h. Canada |

Learners with hearing impairment—not deafness—may need a differentiated way to focus and often benefit from a sound amplification system, which in turn can help all students heighten their attention to instruction. This differentiated presentation allows the deaf student heightened engagement, which capitalizes on his or her residual hearing instead of constantly asking for words, sentences, directions, and explanations to be repeated. The Institute for Enhanced Classroom Hearing (n.d.) purports that students with auditory processing difficulties, learners with attentive and behavioral differences, and students with normal hearing also benefit from sound enhancement systems.

❯ Increase Academic Achievements and Social Participation

Practical approaches that increase academic and social participation include the following examples:

- Peers and staff face students when they speak.
- Classrooms are set up with a circular seating arrangement during discussions (if students are speech reading).
- A normal conversational tone is used without overly enunciating.
- Curriculum-related visuals, outlines, and graphic organizers are used more often.
- Notes (including those from visual presentations) and schedules are offered in advance.
- Individual student conferences are held regularly.

- Appropriate technology (e.g., sound-field amplification systems, captioned videos, computer-assisted instruction, interactive whiteboards, web cameras, hearing aids, visually vibrating devices, infrared systems that use light waves to transmit sound to special light sensitive receivers, video relay services that convert verbal messages into sign language, text telephones that convert verbal responses into text) is used inside and outside the classroom to optimize learner potential and increase participation, communication, and understanding.
- Peers are educated on how and when to assist their classmates (e.g., peer mentors).
- Vocabulary is accompanied with visual cues and gestures.
- Realistic levels of self-efficacy and self-advocacy (e.g., learning logs, social journals, "I can" statements) are established.
- Student interests are inserted into lessons.
- Social inclusion is considered in all school and extracurricular activities.

❍ Know Your Partners

It is imperative to invite and embrace collaboration with related service providers, including sign interpreters, teachers of the deaf, audiologists, speech-language pathologists, guidance counselors, interpreters, transliterators, and, if available, Communication Access Realtime Translation (CART) providers who translate an audio feed with phonetic shorthand on steno machines. CART, often referred to as real-time captioning, can display spoken words as text with devices such as a notebook computer (National Association of the Deaf, n.d.). Educational audiologists and teachers of the deaf provide vital information about the maintenance and calibration of hearing assistive devices to students, staff, and families (Educational Audiology Association, 2015). They may also train teachers and other academic staff on listening checks and offer vital information beyond the student's individualized education program (IEP) meetings to preteach, support, and review academic materials. General and special education teachers should thus share their lesson plans and supportive materials for upcoming units of study with these specialists. Increased home-school partnerships are valuable, too, regardless of family perspectives about supports. Collaboration with families to share strategies, honor perspectives, and maximize the student's academic retention is nonnegotiable.

I was fortunate enough to share my resource classroom with a teacher of the deaf. Through our years together, I watched this professional—who was also deaf—transform both herself and the students she instructed. She collaborated with all staff and was very often the intermediary who negotiated the appropriate accommodations for students with deafness and hearing impairment within the general education classroom. After receiving a cochlear transplant, she was quite annoyed by extraneous sounds that she had never heard before but were now part of her environment (e.g., the beeping that signaled the custodians, the inordinately long morning announcements). Hence, each student who is hearing impaired or deaf has his or her own level of comfort and degree of embracing auditory stimuli and tools, based on prior experiences, family preferences, and personal interest.

Knowing the preferences and abilities of students accessing services means that all staff, families, and students receive the clear message that good instructional practices raise the bar for all learners. Deafness or a hearing impairment does not affect intelligence, but the type of services delivered and the knowledge and partnerships of the school interventionists do affect school performance.

To sum up, it's important to be an advocate for your students with deafness and hearing impairments by

- Valuing explicit instruction.
- Providing appropriate scaffolding.
- Differentiating instruction without diluting objectives.
- Increasing academic achievements.
- Promoting social participation.
- Partnering with staff, specialists, families, and students.

References

Benedict, B. (n.d.) *Hands and voices: Deaf culture and community.* Available: www.handsandvoices.org/comcon/articles/deafculture.htm

Deaf Child Worldwide. (2016). Causes of deafness. Available: www.deafchildworldwide.info/childhood_deafness/causes_of.html

Educational Audiology Association. (2015). Supporting students who are deaf and hard of hearing: Recommended roles of educational audiologists and teachers of the deaf and hard of hearing. Available: www.edaud.org/position-stat/11-position-08-15.pdf

Hallahan, D., Kaufman, J., & Pullen, P. (2012). *Exceptional learners* (12th ed.). Upper Saddle River, NJ: Pearson.

Hearing Loss Association of America. (2016). Types, causes, and treatment. Available: www.hearingloss.org/content/types-causes-and-treatment

Institute for Enhanced Classroom Hearing. (n.d.). The following people benefit from sound enhancement systems. Available: www.classroomhearing.org/research/who.html

National Association of the Deaf. (n.d.). Communication across realtime translation. Available: https://nad.org/issues/technology/captioning/cart

U.S. Department of Education. (2015). *Deaf students' education services*. Available: www2.ed.gov/about/offices/list/ocr/docs/hq9806.html

Professional Resources

Collaborative for Communication Access via Captioning: http://ccacaptioning.org/faqs-cart

Deaf Child Worldwide: www.deafchildworldwide.info

Gallaudet University: www.gallaudet.edu/rsia/world-deaf-information-resource/deaf-information-resources.html

Hearing Loss Association of America: www.hearingloss.org/content/education

Listening and Spoken Language Knowledge Center: www.agbell.org/Tertiary.aspx?id=1237

11

Students with Blindness and Visual Impairments

The Possible Whys

There are multiple causes and types of blindness and vision impairment. Causes include premature birth, a family history of retinoblastoma (cancer of the eye that occurs in children under age 5), congenital cataracts, infection during pregnancy, problems with the central nervous system, seizures, cerebral palsy, hydrocephaly (fluid buildup in the brain), and developmental delay that can lead to visual impairments. Infants born prematurely can develop a severe eye problem called retinopathy of prematurity, which can impair vision and cause legal blindness. Other conditions attributable to vision loss include infections, genetic or metabolic diseases, damage to the brain, and neurological visual impairment (American Foundation for the Blind, 2016b; Center for Parent Information and Resources, 2015; United Cerebral Palsy, 2016).

Vision problems can be refractive ones, meaning that the eye does not bend light properly and results in blurred vision. Nearsightedness (myopia) affects our ability to see things far away, and farsightedness (hyperopia) affects our ability to see objects close-up. Astigmatism is a curvature of the front surface of the eye and causes blurry vision. Students may also have muscular differences such as strabismus, where the eyes cannot focus and look in different directions or turn inward, or nystagmus, which causes involuntary rapid eye movements.

Characteristics and Strengths

The degree and severity with which students exhibit blindness or vision problems can vary greatly, along with the impact on their academic, developmental, and social domains. Learners with low vision may hold papers and objects closer, squint, blink, and rub their eyes often. Students with nearsightedness, farsightedness, and astigmatism usually wear glasses and/or contacts. With this in mind, students may display different facial expressions and need assistance with alternative strategies to pick up on nonverbal language. Students with both severe blindness and intellectual disability can exhibit behaviors such as rocking or twirling.

Classroom Implications

There are special schools for students who are blind, with smaller class sizes, but some critics believe that their academic demands are not as rigorous and put students who are educated in a separate school at a loss for gainful employment since they lack knowledge and skills (AFB, 2016c). Together, as with other differences, educational school teams and families decide on the best placement, whether that is the general education classroom, a self-contained setting, a special school, or a combination of services and supports. Each placement carries with it its own set of advantages and disadvantages.

Learners who are blind or have other visual impairments capitalize on their other senses; they therefore rely more on touching, hearing, smelling, and moving to enhance learning. However, not all students who are blind or have low vision perform better through auditory means (Cowan, n.d.). Braille instruction is provided to students who are blind, with text and ancillary materials translated into Braille ahead of time. If students have low vision, then print is magnified. However, it's important to review what is enlarged, since illustrations, graphs, charts, and other visuals may become distorted when enlarged.

Orientation and mobility (O&M) instruction is a related individualized service. Orientation helps a student know where he or she is and where he or she wants to be. Mobility assists with safely moving from one place to another, whether walking down a school hallway to the next class, crossing a street, getting on a bus, navigating the playground, crossing the stage during a school play or assembly, or participating safely in a physical education class or science lab. In addition, teachers of the visually impaired offer expertise on the classroom strategies and resources that these students need. Services occur within and outside the classroom as needed to assist with school navigation and classroom routines to better pick up cues from the environment (Willings, 2015).

Inclusion Strategies

❯ Encourage Practice, Application, and Independence

Students with visual disabilities or blindness need to develop resiliency and independence. Working backward, staff need to consider the scaffolding necessary to help make that independence happen. A student with low vision often requires increased response time during instruction and assessments or a handheld copy of instructions before he or she independently and accurately completes a task. An assessment given in the morning to a learner with low vision is a better option if that student experiences increased eye fatigue by the afternoon. Categorizing a word list, providing accompanying images, or introducing vocabulary digitally with a speech tool activated to pronounce each word are appropriate accommodations. Additional discussion, more distinct images, and opportunities for guided explorations increase successful application that promotes more independence. Providing a digital book-shelf with audiobooks across the disciplines also helps increase both academic competencies and independence.

Students who have another disability besides visual impairment require comprehensive considerations to differentiate their inclusion strategies. If a student is deaf-blind, then it is vital to provide meaningful and predictable activities with opportunities for interaction and initiation with age-level peers who can also be mentors. Although all students benefit from structured and predictable routines, they are imperative for a student who is deaf-blind since they both reduce stress levels and increase behavioral regulation and participation (Nelson, Greenfield, Hyte, & Shaffer, 2013). A student with albinism is more sensitive to light differences and requires associated adaptations (e.g., time to adjust to classroom light if coming from outside). If a student has an intellectual disability in addition to blindness, then the degree of supports will be more intensive and require increased practice and step-by-step task analysis to promote retention.

❯ Be Environmentally Proactive

Proactive environmental strategies minimize frustrations for both the student and the teacher. Try to see the environment from your student's point of view to recognize potential challenges and then honor his or her personalized accommodations. Provide preferred seating in a more central classroom location within a group of students (Cowan, n.d.). This setup lessens eye strain and encourages social inclusion. A student may be more comfortable away from a light source such as a window or hall-way light. Allow the student to explore the classroom and orient himself or herself before other students fill the room, and provide an opportunity to request any physical rearrangements necessary to increase mobility.

Dimming the lights in the classroom, covering a desk or workspace with dark-colored paper, and preparing less cluttered assessments on colored paper are all ways to reduce glare, offer visual contrast, and help increase focus. A student may also need a larger desk for additional materials and access to an electrical outlet for specialized equipment. Specialized equipment (e.g., wheelchair, specialized lighting, AAC device, voice synthesizer) is always a consideration for students with disabilities if the nature of the disability warrants such a service.

◉ Value Verbal, Tactile, and Tech Tools

Offer step-by-step oral narration of directions and written materials, including descriptions of novel or visual content. As appropriate, have materials provided in advance in Braille (for those students who can take advantage of it), including worksheets across the curriculum, texts, science lab instructions, novels, supplementary math aids, and labels. Offer younger students developmentally appropriate material with different pacing, expectations, and supports, such as modeling how to firmly press fingers and related Braille literacy materials (Hudson, n.d.).

Other accommodations as specified in a learner's individualized education program (IEP) may include, but are not limited to, more verbal direction, large-print books, magnified pages, voice-activated computers, and vocabulary placed on individual cards with raised illustrations and contextual sentences to better associate vocabulary with larger ideas. When teaching an abstract concept, such as the concepts of meiosis and mitosis in a high school science class, provide symbolic representation in tangible forms that students can hold and touch. Cell division, for example, can be represented with tools such as pipe cleaners and beads in glass jars. Elementary students can form spelling words in shaving cream or in salt trays to offer tactile elements that imprint memory of visually displayed information.

Technological supports for students with blindness and low vision include screen readers, video services, Braille note-takers, talking calculators, voice-over features on a computer that give spoken descriptions, an audio ball (a bell inside a ball tossed in physical education), a talking thermometer, electronic speaking dictionaries, raised tactile drawings, and algebra tiles with additional modifications to specify color distinctions. Mobile tablets or other electronic or computer-assisted devices can be activated for speech capabilities. CaptiNarrator (www.captivoice.com/capti-site) is an app that takes text from the Internet and puts it on a playlist so students can hear words from the sites. This helps students with visual impairment, students who speak another language (since it also translates words), and students with dyslexia. Desktop scanners have optical character recognition software that increases reading independence by converting text and scanned images into machine readable text. The app BeSpecular (www.bespecular.com) allows students with a visual impairment to take pictures, dictate audio requests on clarification of images, and relay this information to volunteers who describe what the images represent.

Low-tech tools include modified board games that allow access—for example, checkers with squared and round shapes to indicate the difference between red and black pieces or a tactile Scrabble set. It is vital that modified resources aren't limited to just textbooks but include all learning materials. Access to a classroom game such as checkers teaches turn taking and critical thinking skills. A tactile map is a three-dimensional accommodation to preview and navigate a student's route, such as hallway transitions or a trip to the restroom. A GPS navigation app can store frequent locations and is available in multiple languages. Whether you offer low- or high-tech tools, individualize their use to optimize your student's performance.

❯ Educate Peers and Adults

It is important for peers to know that students with blindness and low vision may have different ways of seeing but can be academically on par and often have usable vision that needs to be acknowledged. Whether a student uses a cane, assistive technology, or extra verbal directions, expectations should never be lowered. Both peers and staff need to view this visual difference as just that: a difference, not a deficiency or level of incompetency. Students with visual disabilities should participate in all whole-class and cooperative learning group activities, as well as extracurricular activities such as band, chorus, clubs, and sports.

❯ Keep Your Eyes on the Outcomes

When appropriate accommodations and modifications are available, students who are blind or have visual impairment with low vision can achieve the same learning outcomes as peers who are sighted (American Foundation for the Blind, 2016a). Keeping the outcomes in mind means that structured objectives are offered with individualized adaptations and are shared with students and families. If more assistance is required with orientation and mobility, then consult specialists, vision rehabilitation therapists, or low-vision therapists.

It is okay not to know all of the necessary strategies, but it is not okay to ignore the outcomes you are helping your students achieve. If you plan a car trip and get lost, you don't just abandon the trip—you stop and ask for directions or use a navigation tool. Students with low vision and blindness require a resilient and positive attitude that acknowledges different roads to their destination. As Helen Keller stated, "The only thing worse than being blind is having sight but no vision."

To sum up this chapter on low vision and blindness, it's important to consider

- The value of practice, application, and independence.
- Proactively arranged environments.
- Verbal, tactile, and technological adaptations customized for the student's needs.
- Education of peers and staff.
- A positive view toward successful outcomes.

References

American Foundation for the Blind (AFB). (2016a). *Accommodations and modifications at a glance: Educational accommodations for students who are blind or visually impaired.* Available: www.afb.org/info/programs-and-services/professional-development/experts-guide/accommodations-and-modifications-at-a-glance/1235

American Foundation for the Blind. (2016b). Eye conditions. Available: www.afb.org/info/living-with-vision-loss/eye-conditions/12

American Foundation for the Blind. (2016c). Specialized education services for students with vision loss. Available: www.afb.org/info/programs-and-services/public-policy-center/specialized-services/specialized-education-services-for-students-with-vision-loss/1235

Center for Parent Information and Resources. (2015). Visual impairment, including blindness. Available: www.parentcenterhub.org/repository/visualimpairment/

Cowan, C. (n.d.) *Possible accommodations for the student with a visual impairment.* Texas School for the Blind and Visually Impaired. Available: www.tsbvi.edu/instructional-resources/3657-vision-accommodations

Hudson, L. (n.d.). Teaching Braille to young children. *Paths to Literacy.* Available: www.pathstoliteracy.org/teaching-braille-young-children

Nelson, C., Greenfield. R. Hyte, H., & Shaffer, J. (2013). Stress, behavior, and children and youth who are deafblind. *Research and Practice for Persons with Severe Disabilities, 38*(3), 139–156.

United Cerebral Palsy. (2016). What are the causes of vision loss? What puts a child at risk? Available: www.mychildwithoutlimits.org/understand/vision-loss/what-are-the-causes-of-vision-loss

Willings, C. (2015). Teaching students with visual impairments. Orientation and mobility specialist. Available: www.teachingvisuallyimpaired.com/orientation—mobility-specialist.html

Professional Resources

AFB *Access World* magazine: www.afb.org/aw/main.asp

American Association of Blind Teachers: www.blindteachers.net

BeSpecular: www.bespecular.com

Bookshare: www.bookshare.org/cms

Deaf-Blind Education: www.deafblindinfo.org

Enrichment Audio Resources Center: www.earsforeyes.info

Iris Center. (2016). Accommodations to the physical environment: Setting up a classroom for students with visual impairments. Available: http://iris.peabody.vanderbilt.edu/module/v01-clearview

My Child Without Limits. (2016). What are the causes of vision loss? What puts a child at risk? Available: www.mychildwithoutlimits.org/understand/vision-loss/what-

National Alliance of Blind Students: www.blindstudents.org

National Federation of the Blind: https://nfb.org

Perkins Scout. (n.d.). Causes of blindness and visual impairment. Available: www.perkinselearning.org/scout/causes-blindness-and-visual-impairment

Vision Aware. (2016). An introduction to orientation and mobility skills. Available: www.visionaware.org/info/everyday-living/essential-skills/an-introduction-to-orientation-and-mobility-skills/123

Willings, C. (n.d.). School adaptations: Teaching students with visual impairments. Available: www.teachingvisuallyimpaired.com/adapt.html

12
Students with Physical Disabilities

The Possible Whys

Physical disabilities can occur from accidents; substance and child abuse; neuromotor impairments such as cerebral palsy, spina bifida, and brain injury; or diseases such as poliomyelitis or bone tuberculosis (Disabled World, 2016; Project IDEAL, 2013). Neuromotor impairments affect the function of the brain, spinal cord, and nervous system, and impulses sent to the muscles are affected. Physical impairments can occur before, during, or after birth. Fetal alcohol syndrome, juvenile rheumatoid arthritis, seizures, and AIDS are additional causes. Therefore, etiology is genetic or acquired with neuromuscular, orthopedic, musculoskeletal, and other health impairments as possible causes (Center for Parent Information and Resources, 2015; Education Encyclopedia, 2016).

Characteristics and Strengths

If a learner with a physical impairment receives an IDEA classification, then he or she is usually placed under the category of Orthopedic Impairment or the broader category classification of Other Health Impairment (OHI). Characteristics will vary from student to student, but intelligence has the same full range as for students without physical disabilities. Physical characteristics are dependent on extremities impacted (e.g., quadriplegia, paraplegia) and on types of movements with spasticity (tight or stiff muscles with an imbalance of signals from the central nervous system), choreoathetoid (uncontrollable movements), and atonic (lapse in muscle tone, with seizures evidenced). In addition, students with physical differences may also have other classifications. Other possible conditions include seizures, spina bifida, orthopedic and muscular differences, muscular dystrophy, juvenile rheumatoid arthritis, scoliosis, fragile X syndrome, and spinal muscular atrophy (Handicaps Welfare Association, n.d.). Fine- and/or gross-motor skills are also affected, with fine-motor differences having an impact on the muscles in the hands and wrists. A range of behavioral and learning characteristics accompanies physical differences, including weaker and stronger modalities, different interests, and varying levels of academic performance.

Classroom Implications

Physical differences and the condition's severity influence student stamina, which in turn affects school performance and behavior (e.g., decreased attention span, lower retention, restlessness). Educational progress and social skill development are affected if a student must be hospitalized frequently or miss school for long periods of time. If a student needs to receive medical attention in the school setting (e.g., catheterization), then the appropriate school health personnel such as a school nurse is involved. Always keep an eye on safety factors for the student with and without a physical disability. Be certain to provide accommodations that honor the student's level of performance, interest, and stamina, without diluting curriculum expectations. Students with other health impairments, such as asthma, diabetes, and epilepsy, have specific needs about which classroom teachers need to be knowledgeable. Teachers also need to be in communication with and collaborate with families, school nurses, physicians, physical therapists, behavior interventionists, and other related service providers so they can discuss safety, medication, routines, and best practices. In addition, note that a student with ADHD may receive a classification of OHI (see Chapter 2 for specific characteristics, classroom implications, inclusion strategies, and resources).

Inclusion Strategies
❍ Explore and Create Tools

Learn how to effectively include any adaptive devices the student with physical disabilities might use (e.g., alternative keyboards, computer control switches, a voice recorder, a cushioned chair, hearing and/or vision devices, adaptive scissors, alternative writing tools, slant boards). Try low-tech options to help these students, too. As examples, tape a writing composition paper to a student desk so it does not move if the student does not have a steady hand, or ask a custodian to lower or raise a desk to accommodate wheelchair height as appropriate. Try using a turkey baster instead of an eyedropper in a science lab, which may be easier for the student to hold and manipulate if fine-motor skills are affected. Provide a cushion or beanbag for seating.

Allow students to get messy and construct their learning on an instructional—not frustration—level.

Diverse resources, strategies, and materials include, but are not limited to, using modeling clay to practice squeezing, using larger writing tools to increase hand stamina, or making differently sized pencil grips available. It is not always about giving students the answers; it is also vital to allow students to take learning risks so they can explore and gain knowledge inside textbooks and through experiences in their environments. This will help them own the knowledge. Students with physical and other health impairments may need additional help, but offering too much help thwarts their independence and can enable learners. Address any visual-spatial problems that are evidenced by offering puzzles, art, building blocks, and figure-ground activities to better see an object against a busy background. When visual skills are strengthened, the increased attention to detail is transferred across the disciplines to achieve academic demands in reading, math, science, social studies, and other content areas. Some coordination difficulties can be addressed by simply offering instruction at different paces or with additional time to complete tasks (since students have less stamina and require more frequent breaks).

➲ Integrate Academic Goals with Functional Ones

Adhere to the goals delineated in each student's individualized education program (IEP). Focus on how to integrate academic goals with functional ones. For example, a teacher who selects a nonfiction passage on Internet safety, rather than one on circus animals, can still show students how to extract the main idea and draw inferences from written material but do so with stronger relevancy to life skills. The circus choice, although a fun one, serves no functional purpose. Collaboratively weigh and review options, considering age levels and relevancy to real-world experiences and plans to safely increase independence. It is also important for students to know how to share responsibilities in a cooperative group assignment, ask for help, and transition from one activity to the next.

A student who hones addition and subtraction skills by focusing on deposits and withdrawals made to a checking account is practicing a functional math skill that promotes increased independence. Personal development and confidence are achieved though math and reading assignments that are infused with concepts centered around art, financial responsibility, dietary choices, exercise, music, and other relevant topics that promote increased independence. This is essential for all students but especially for a learner with a physical disability who may have more difficulty with navigation and less prior experience.

Remember, too, physical differences do not mean that students should be excused from developing skills that involve waiting one's turn in class discussions, completing an assignment by a given due date, or interacting appropriately with peers and adults. By not treating these students differently from your other students, you are also modeling for the whole class the respect and tolerance all students deserve.

❯ Reach Out to the Team

Collaborate with specialists—social workers and physical, speech-language, and occupational therapists—who may already know your student with physical disabilities. Seek out the valuable insights families can provide, and tap them as academic partners, especially if a student misses school because of his or her physical disability. You can do this by sharing instructional materials so their child can make up or keep up with schoolwork.

Enlist the student's classmates to help promote a supportive team mentality. Peers can also serve as academic tutors and facilitate social interactions within the classroom and during extracurricular activities. Always model respectful relationships that are founded on multiple capabilities and means of expression—not physical limitations.

Often, peers require increased sensitivity around a classmate with physical disabilities. Inviting inspiring people from the community to visit your classroom might be helpful. As the coordinator for a school disability awareness program, I arranged for a speaker with cerebral palsy and ADHD to speak with students in grades 2–6. He began his talk by telling the students that they could ask him any question they wanted. The following questions are just a few of the many asked, but they offer a glimpse into how young students may perceive someone with a disability:

- What kind of disabilities do your friends have?
- Do you wish you could walk?
- Can you play video games?

The guest speaker responded that he is happy being who he is and would not change a thing. When he shared that some of his friends use a wheelchair and other assistive devices to help them move around but that most of his friends do not have a physical disability and that he likes to play video games, the students' eyes grew wide. They were equally enthralled when they saw a Harley Davidson bumper sticker on the back of his wheelchair. For these students, the point was underscored that everyone moves at different speeds and has varying academic, social, and behavioral likes and dislikes—not just people with physical disabilities.

This example emphasizes how imperative it is for both educators and students not to make assumptions about a student with a physical disability. Think about how his or her characteristics are perceived by others to maximize everyone's strengths and abilities.

❯ Be a Catalyst Who Helps, Monitors, and Fades Support

Help, but do not enable. Offer cue cards and adaptations, but also have a plan to safely fade support by consulting the experts on your team, as described in the previous sections. A gradual release of responsibility is based on progress achieved. Just as supports are incremental, allow the learner to continually increase his or her skills and confidence to complete tasks. Provide an inviting environment with a desk arrangement that expands mobility and avoids physical or psychological exclusion. Honor strengths, but do not allow mobility issues to limit school successes with both academics and socialization. Be an advocate for how to remove the barriers for students with physical differences.

Andrew Wyeth, in his painting *Christina's World,* portrayed a neighbor of his relaxed in a field. He painted the beauty of each blade of grass and the woman's gaze as she looks forward. Many people who do not know the background of this picture are surprised when they learn that the real-life Christina crawled into the field each day since she had limited mobility. She was a courageous young woman who did not want the help of others and was determined to exhibit independence. Wyeth's Christina can offer insights for school staff to also view and portray students with physical differences in positive lights.

To sum up, it's important to remember that students with physical differences

- Thrive in inviting spaces and among people with positive attitudes.
- Respond to creative tools that help but do not enable.
- Have many strengths and are not defined by their limitations.
- Require self-advocacy and continuous steps toward independence.
- Are equal members of the school team and broader community.

References

Center for Parent Information and Resources. (2015). Other health impairment. Available: www.parentcenterhub.org/repository/ohi/

Disabled World. (2016). Physical and mobility impairments: Information and news. Available: www.disabled-world.com/disability/types/mobility

Education Encyclopedia. (2016). Education of individuals with physical disabilities: Types and causes of physical disabilities: The basics and history of special education, trends and controversies. Available: http://education.stateuniversity.com/pages/2322/Physical-Disabilities-Education-Individuals-With.html

Handicaps Welfare Association. (n.d.). General information on physical disabilities. Available: http://hwa.org.sg/news/general-information-on-physical-disabilities

Project IDEAL. (2013). Orthopedic impairments. Available: www.projectidealonline.org/v/orthopedic-impairments

Professional Resources

Adapted Physical Education National Standards: www.apens.org/whatisape.html

Cerebral Palsy Guide (2016). Spastic cerebral palsy. Available: www.cerebralpalsyguide.com/cerebral-palsy/types/spastic

PE Central, Adaptive Physical Education Resources: www.pecentral.org/adapted/adaptedmenu.html

United Cerebral Palsy: http://ucp.org

13
Students with Multiple Abilities

The Possible Whys

Staff members need to honor a learner's inner core to value and capitalize on what each student can do. Weaker characteristics exist in all learners, whether they have an individualized education program (IEP), a 504 plan, a communication profile, or a set of behavioral interventions. However, an instructional view that values a strength paradigm highlights student skill sets and appreciates each learner's unique qualities as they interact with academic content, peers, and adults in their school and home environments. For example, Willis (2007) points out that the *L* in LD refers to *learning*, but the *D* often has multiple meanings—from *difference* to *deficiency* to *disability*. The intention of this resource, however, is to support educators as they strive to help an incredibly wide range of students achieve their learning goals, despite the differences they exhibit, whether they are emotional, social, behavioral, cognitive, physical, communicative, sensory, cultural, racial, or a combination of two or more characteristics. Chuck Close, an artist who has dyslexia and partial paralysis, purports that you should never let anyone define what you are capable of by using parameters that don't apply to you.

Students have different ability levels and mitigating factors, which include varying levels of home support; a range of attention spans; different levels of neural activity; premature birth; a lack of oxygen at birth; chromosomal differences; genetic disorders; accidents; infections; and physical, social, behavioral, and emotional impairment, along with the specific causes for each of the disabilities referenced in prior chapters.

Characteristics and Strengths

Having multiple disabilities means that a learner has more than one disability, but it does not indicate the number, type, or severity of those disabilities (Center for Parent Information and Resources, 2015). Combinations of learning, social, emotional, behavioral, physical, speech/language, and sensory differences constitute multiple disabilities. Students with multiple disabilities often have associated medical conditions. For example, a learner with traumatic brain injury may also have an emotional difference or asthma, whereas a student with an orthopedic impairment may also have autism, deafness, or blindness. There is no template for the characteristics that a student with multiple disabilities displays. As with other differences, it's critical to identify and tap into individual learners' strengths. It is vital to remember that students with singular and multiple disabilities also have multiple abilities.

Classroom Implications

The differences exhibited among students with disabilities influence the specially designed instruction that is offered. Such students often require support with learning, remembering, applying new information, speaking, listening, communicating, concentrating, and performing self-care and daily functional tasks. As for all students, considerations are given to provide age-appropriate and grade-level adaptations. At times, students may only partially participate in a task that is beyond their instructional level or level of physical safety. In addition, be sure to value social, emotional, and academic growth, providing encouragement to work alongside peers. Figuring out who each student is means that teachers must take a deeper look at their students —beyond their surface labels—and not simply focus on their differences from preschool through high school.

Inclusion Strategies
❯ Intervene Early and Frequently

Staff need to attach instructional strategies to their knowledge of their students, subject matter, and situations (Marzano, 2009). Marzano goes on to say that instructional, management, and assessment strategies exist in a constellation. One cannot assume that the same strategy allows each student to shine. It is important to note that this resource offers research-based strategies to increase student outcomes, but educators work in that laboratory called a school, with variables known as students. The same strategy—even though it may be evidence-based practice—may have a negative effect on one student while yielding positive outcomes for another.

For example, a student who exhibits defiant behavior may be discomforted by an inordinate number of classroom rules, whereas a student with ADHD may appreciate a stricter framework to better manage his or her behavior. This does not mean that a student with defiant behavior should not be given rules to follow, but it does mean that knowledge of that student shapes the communication and feedback that will achieve a greater internal structure to follow external realities. Offering graphic organizers to take notes can be differentiated for a student who is blind, a learner with auditory processing difficulties, and a student with dyslexia. Offering positive feedback is important, but again it should be uniquely designed and on an appropriate level for individual students, whether they have a learning, emotional, or communicative difference or a combination of abilities.

Hattie (2012) outlines best practices that value clear models, individual and whole-class feedback, formative assessment, and increased student ownership. Early and frequent structured interventions are essential with research-based and developmentally and age-appropriate practices. Many forms of assistive technology are available, such as an augmentative or alternative communication; adaptive switches; specialized desks; a laptop with alternative ways to input information; a mobile tablet with accessibility tools to compensate for vision, hearing, physical, motor, and learning disabilities; a slant board; a pencil with a modified grip; or a digital pen to record information. Students may require significant modifications that help but do not enable, and their IEPs will note which ones are required.

❂ Frame the Outcomes

The varying academic, behavioral, social, emotional, communication, sensory, and physical levels that a student with disabilities displays influence the type, intensity, and duration of the strategies and interventions you should employ. Overall, a structured inclusive environment offers consistency, predictability, and reinforcement to modify, teach, and strengthen desired outcomes across the academic domains. That consistency occurs within a structured framework: lesson plans. Quarterly, monthly, weekly, and daily mapping of goals and outcomes helps educators and—consequently—their learners (Karten, 2010). Fisher and Frey (2011) maintain that the purpose of a lesson is connected to a theme, problem, project, or question that offers students meaning and connections. Staff agendas need to honor diverse student realities and offer a framework of rigorous expectations that is accompanied by adaptations that value the diversity of student levels found in the classroom. Outcomes need to be framed to value the discrete steps learners make toward partial mastery. The achievement of 100 percent mastery is an evolutionary process.

A step-by-step approach to achieving these outcomes might resemble the following:

Step 1: Establish positive attitudes.

Step 2: Engage in collaborative organization and inquiry.

Step 3: Value data: observe, analyze, and respond with the appropriate interventions.

Step 4: Strengthen your relationships and programs.

Step 5: Reflect.

◉ Provide Strategy-Rich Environments

Learners may need help to remember and apply previously learned skills; interact appropriately with peers and adults; increase self-efficacy; display sustained attention; and manage anxiety, stress, and fatigue. The inclusive classroom needs to provide a strategy-filled environment that offers alternative ways for learners to access information, communicate needs, and navigate daily routines to achieve high expectations (see CAST, 2015, for approaches). For example, a language-rich classroom allows various forms of communication (e.g., assistive devices, vocabulary lists, sign language) and an emphasis on functional skills, such as ordering from a menu and reading a movie schedule. Ongoing study skills teach learners how to access and better remember information. Students with different ability skill sets, from preschool to high school, may not know the answer to every question posed, but they need to know how to access help and—ultimately—help themselves find those answers. This means knowing who can assist and the type of supports needed. Learners are unique, and so too are staff. Knowing where and when to help—but not enable—students means observing and responding to them with strategies that lead them to reflect on and own the strategies.

Infuse academic instruction with daily activities and student interests. As an example, if a student with autism who also has a learning disability with weak mathematical reasoning and lower language skills loves butterflies, offer her "butterflied" supports. Allow her to count and talk about butterflies. Ask her to examine the patterns on butterflies' wings when learning about symmetry in math, research the stages of a butterfly, or write a play that has a butterfly as a protagonist.

Self-Management: "I Do, You Do, We Do, They Do"

Self-management plans are designed to teach students to complete tasks independently and take an active role to monitor and reinforce their own behavior (University of Kansas, n.d.). For students with different ability levels, this is accomplished through individualized release of responsibility, monitoring, communication, and reinforcement. Although the gradual release of responsibility is often presented as "I do, we do, you do it together, you do it alone" (Fisher & Frey, 2008), Figure 13.1 differentiates the process with the sequencing of steps and the addition of "they do."

Figure 13.1 | Self-Management

I Do	You Do	We Do	They Do

Since constructivist approaches place an emphasis on knowledge construction, rather than knowledge reproduction (Trinity College, 2002), this tool is modified to offer a gradual release of responsibility to help each individual maximize his or her potential and to facilitate collaboration. The first step—*I do*—sees the teacher offer the necessary modeling with minimal direction, which is intended to invoke critical thinking skills, not mere replication, during the second step of *you do*. The third step—*we do*—invites class discussion and group reflection. Finally, *they do* means that the task is independently, cooperatively, and consistently completed.

For example, a teacher models how to diagram a novel's plot, and then students delve into it independently before coming back together as a group to share discoveries. The last step is added to note that their literary skills are indeed theirs—not ones that belong to staff. The scaffolding required is intended to be faded with increased learner discovery, reflection, and self-management to construct greater responsibility.

❯ Collaboration Between Educators and Students

The "I Do, You Do, We Do, They Do" model can be applied from the early grades through high school. For example, educators can show preschoolers how to transition from one activity to the next. After repeated individual and cooperative practice, individual students—and the class as a whole—transition between activities when a cue (such as music) is played. Finally, with monitoring and reinforcement, the transition becomes a class norm. Likewise, a math teacher who offers direct instruction on how to convert mixed numbers into improper fractions to perform area and perimeter calculations is demonstrating the first step (*I do*). Afterward, the learners perform fraction conversions on their own during independent practice (*You do*), and then students experience guided practice as needed with peer modeling and interactions (*We do*). Finally, when students achieve mastery as noted on assessments, they own the concepts and strategies to solve the area and perimeter problems independently (*They do*).

❯ Collaboration Among Educators, Families, and Students

This approach can incorporate families when the goal is one that involves them in some way, such as finishing a research or book report, developing a consistent plan for the student to complete and return homework, or learning effective time management skills. For example, educators share the appropriate content from their class with families on a weekly basis via a teacher website or printed newsletter (*I do*). Follow-up includes ideas for a continuation of the learning at home (*You do*). Collaboration and ongoing communication should continue to take place among educators, families, and students to monitor students' progress toward their goals in the home environment (*We do*). Finally, students own the skills to conceptualize and complete tasks independently in both home and school settings (*They do*).

❯ Collaboration Among Administrators, Staff, and Students

This approach can also incorporate administrators. For example, administration shares lesson strategies for differentiation of instruction. The professional development goals are designed to guide staff on a path to personalize concepts and skills based on diverse learner needs and skill sets. The *I do* step includes a model of how to vary activities, infuse technology, and effectively implement competency-based instruction with data. Next, the *you do* step allows both general and special education staff, along with specialists and related service providers, to plan units and lessons that implement personalized strategies. The *we do* step is achieved when staff guide students to complete academic tasks and be aware of individual learning goals. This step may also include increased staff-student and administration-staff conferencing to ensure accurate, reflective, and ongoing self-regulation. Finally, the *they do* step is when teachers observe that students and staff are able to independently self-regulate.

When a learner self-regulates, he or she is aware of the next steps and responsible actions required with an approach that fine-tunes academics and behavior based on increased reflections. The idea is not to record learning goals and performance data, which can be anecdotal, observational, or written, but to allow learners to actively formulate, regulate, and own the strategies to achieve ongoing successes.

References

CAST. (2015). About universal design for learning. Available: www.cast.org/our-work/about-udl.html

Center for Parent Information and Resources. (2015). *Multiple disabilities.* Newark, NJ: Author. Available: www.parentcenterhub.org/repository/multiple

Fisher, D., & Frey, N. (2008). *Better learning through structured teaching: A framework for the gradual release of responsibility.* Alexandria, VA: ASCD.

Fisher, D., & Frey, N. (2011). *The purposeful classroom: How to structure lessons with learning goals in mind.* Alexandria, VA: ASCD.

Hattie, J. (2012). *Visible learning for teachers.* New York: Routledge.

Karten, T. (2010). *Inclusion lesson plan book for the 21st century.* Naples, FL: National Professional Resources.

Marzano, R. (2009). Setting the record straight on "high-yield" strategies. *Phi Delta Kappan, 91*(1), 30–37.

Trinity College. (2002). Constructivism: Constructivist theory and social development theory. Available: http://cstcd.ie

University of Kansas. (n.d.). Teaching self-management skills. Available: www.specialconnections. ku.edu/?q=behavior_plans/positive_behavior_support_interventions/teacher_tools/teaching_self_management_skills

Willis, J. (2007). *Brain-friendly strategies for the inclusion classroom.* Alexandria, VA: ASCD.

Professional Resources

Apple Accessibility: www.apple.com/accessibility/ios

Center on Technology and Disability: http://ctdinstitute.org

Karten, T. (2016). *Inclusion do's, don'ts, do betters.* Alexandria, VA: ASCD.

Paths to Literacy. Technology for students with multiple disabilities: www.pathstoliteracy.org/technology-students-multiple-disabilities

Appendix A

Capitalize on Strengths

Visuals	• Charts, tables, diagrams, and infographics
	• Comic strips (www.readwritethink.org/classroom-resources/student-interactives/comic-creator-30021.html)
	• Curriculum-related pictures, captioned drawings, wall charts, graphic organizers (http://freeology.com, www.pics4learning.com/)
	• Demonstration (www.teachthought.com/pedagogy/assessment/60-things-students-can-create-to-demonstrate-what-they-know/)
	• Flashcards (www.cram.com, https://quizlet.com/)
	• Gestures (http://leader.pubs.asha.org/article.aspx?articleid=1921130)
	• Highlighting in text
	• Outlines and visual webs (www.inspiration.com/Kidspiration)
	• Timelines (www.dipity.com, www.readwritethink.org/files/resources/interactives/timeline_2/)
	• Video modeling (www.watchmelearn.com/video-modeling/what-is-video-modeling)
	• Videos (https://animoto.com)
	• Visual dictionaries (www.visualdictionaryonline.com)

Continued

Movement	<ul><li>Classroom stations (http://thecornerstoneforteachers.com/free-resources/centers/setting-up-centers)</li><li>Curriculum walks</li><li>Fidget toys or doodling</li><li>Frequent short breaks (www.gonoodle.com)</li><li>Hands-on activities (www.colorincolorado.org/article/hands-activities)</li><li>Physical objects</li><li>Real and virtual manipulatives (http://nlvm.usu.edu/en/nav/vlibrary.html)</li></ul>
Interpersonal activities	<ul><li>Cooperative learning activities (www.colorincolorado.org/article/cooperative-learning-strategies)</li><li>Debates, speeches, conversations, class discussions</li><li>Morning/afternoon/weekly meetings</li><li>Shoulder buddies</li><li>Student presentations</li><li>Think-pair-share (www.readwritethink.org/professional-development/strategy-guides/using-think-pair-share-30626.html)</li></ul>
Listening	<ul><li>Auditory signals (http://wonderteacher.com/auditory-attention-getters-for-classroom-management/)</li><li>Auditory stimulation</li><li>Background music (http://8tracks.com/explore/classroom/hot/1)</li><li>Curriculum-related songs, chants, raps (www.flocabulary.com)</li><li>Discussion</li><li>Prerecorded directions and instruction</li><li>Read-alouds (www.educationworld.com/a_curr/curr213.shtml)</li><li>Verbal analogies (www.wordmasterschallenge.com/listcategory/teaching-analogies)</li><li>Verbal direction and repetition (https://goalbookapp.com/toolkit/goal/following-directions-in-the-classroom)</li></ul>

Appendix B

Strategy-Rich Practices

These interventions are applicable to academic, social, emotional, and behavioral situations for students across ability levels and embrace each learner's individual strengths. In the second column, you are invited to note how a few of these descriptors relate to planning, instruction, and assessment. Offer brief dated comments on the lesson-based evidence for the whole class, small groups, or individual students.

Strategy-Rich Practices	Lesson-Based Evidence
1. Embrace and promote positive attitudes.	
2. Maintain structured and organized environments.	
3. Focus on lesson outcomes and skill sets.	
4. Monitor learner's progress.	
5. Provide realistic, timely, and specific feedback.	
6. Offer direct step-by-step instructions.	
7. Encourage self-efficacy.	
8. Apply student's interests into lessons.	
9. Vary methods of instruction and engagement.	

Continued

Strategy-Rich Practices	Lesson-Based Evidence
10. Introduce lessons in novel, attention-getting ways.	
11. Explore ways to advance attention—not chastise noncompliance.	
12. Encourage self-regulation.	
13. Scaffold as needed within instructional levels.	
14. Keep an eye on when and how to fade support.	
15. Coordinate strategies with staff, families, students, and peers.	
16. Infuse high expectations into your classroom.	
17. Promote strategic learning (e.g., digital notes, mnemonics, calendars, sticky notes) to increase memory, organization, and application of concepts.	
18. Invite active involvement.	
19. Reinforce efforts and mastery.	
20. Know what to do next: strategize, prepare, and review.	

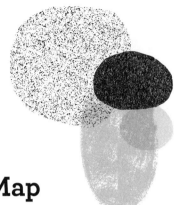

Appendix C

Personalized Learning Map

This organizer is intended as a tool for staff to collaboratively house information on learners, invite more personalized instruction, and review student progress. This learning map outlines a student's level to better individualize instructional learning experiences. It is a working document that is initially filled in by reviewing a student's IEP or 504 plan and noting that learner's annual levels, goals, and skills. This map is also intended for use with learners who receive RTI or multitiered supports. It is also meant to personalize the learning experience for students both with and without RTI plans or IEPs; it can help match individualized needs with the appropriate evidence-based practice. Not every column is filled in, but note that the recognition of learner strengths and interests and the evidence-based practice minimize the challenges. Personalization involves collaborative planning, which continually values student self-regulation from the early primary grades through middle and high school.

Student Information: Age, Grade IEP Classification (if applicable)	
Learner Strengths	
Learner Challenges	
School/Home Interests	
Academic Skills	
Social/Emotional/Behavioral Skills	
Communicative Skills: Speech/Language	

Continued

Physical Skills & Environmental Considerations	
Sensory Skills & Environmental Considerations	
Functional Goals	
Transitional Concerns	
Accommodations	
Modifications	
Self-Regulatory Skills (learners spin the accommodations and modifications into opportunities for growth with increased self-advocacy and ownership of their skills)	
Evidence-Based Practices: MTSS, RTI, UDL, UBD, PBL, DI (multitiered system of supports, response to intervention, universal design for learning, understanding by design, problem/project-based learning, differentiated instruction)	
Resources/Materials/Technology	
Collaborative Partners • Administrative support to maintain and catapult progress (e.g., provision of planning time, resources, materials, professional development, emotional support) • Family support to share strategies, honor perspectives, maximize retention, and send strong same-team philosophy	

• Staff supports and collaboration with related service providers (e.g., coteachers, sign interpreters, teachers of the deaf, audiologists, speech-language pathologists, guidance counselors, occupational and physical therapists, orientation-mobility trainers, behavioral interventionists, social workers, school psychologists, instructional coaches, paraprofessionals, learning consultants, etc.)	
• Peer supports/cooperative partners	
Progress Monitoring (dated comments)	
Recommendations	
Additional Comments:	

Appendix D
Bibliotherapy Choices

The following books are examples of fiction and nonfiction texts for students and adults to gain an increased knowledge of and sensitivity to the perspectives of learners with differences.

Difference	Elementary Level	Upper Elementary/Secondary Level
Autism	*Blue Bottle Mystery* by K. Hoopmann *Elemental Island* by K. Hoopmann *Ian's Walk* by L. Lears *Joey and Sam* by I. Katz *My Brother Charlie* by H. R. Peete and R. Peete *My Friend with Autism* by B. Bishop *Since We're Friends: An Autism Picture Book* by C. Shally and D. Harrington	*Al Capone Does My Shirts* by G. Choldenko *Born on a Blue Day: Inside the Extraordinary Mind of an Autistic Savant* by D. Tammet *The Curious Incident of the Dog in the Night-time* by M. Haddon *House Rules* by J. Picoult *Look Me in the Eye* by J. E. Robison *Mockingbird* by K. Erskine *The Reason I Jump* by N. Higashida *Rogue* by L. Miller-Lachmann *Rules* by C. Lord *The Way I See It* by T. Grandin *A Wizard Alone* by D. Duane

Difference	Elementary Level	Upper Elementary/Secondary Level
Emotional, Social, and Behavioral	*Dude That's Rude!* by P. Espeland *Good Bye Ouchies & Grouchies! Hello Happy Feelings* by L. Namka *How Are You Peeling?* by S. Freymann *Matt the Moody Hermit Crab* by C. McGee *Super Lexi* by E. Lesko *When My Worries Get Too Big! A Relaxation Book for Children Who Live with Anxiety* by K. Buron	*The Adventures of Stretch More-Pick-Your-Path Stories for Solving Problems Together* by T. Epstein and R. Greene *Cool, Calm, and Confident* by L. Schab *The Glass Castle: A Memoir* by J. Walls *The Mindful Teen: Powerful Skills to Help You Handle Stress, One Moment at a Time* by D. Vo *Running with Scissors: A Memoir* by A. Burroughs *Up and Down the Worry Hill* by A. Wagner
ADHD	*All Dogs Have ADHD* by K. Hoopmann *Eagle Eyes* by J. Gehert *Eukee the Jumpy Jumpy Elephant* by C. Corman *Putting on the Brakes: Young Person's Guide to Understanding Attention Deficit Hyperactivity Disorder* by P. Quinn and J. Stern *Shelley the Hyperactive Turtle* by D. Moss	*A Girl's Guide to ADHD: How They Feel and Why They Do What They Do* by K. Nadeau, E. Dixon, and P. Quinn *Joey Pigza Swallowed the Key* by J. Gantos *Learning to Slow Down and Pay Attention: A Book for Kids About ADHD* by C. Beyl *Smart but Scattered: The Revolutionary "Executive Skills" Approach to Helping Kids Reach Their Potential* by P. Dawson *Zipper the Kid with ADHD* by C. Janover

Continued

Difference	Elementary Level	Upper Elementary/Secondary Level
Dyslexia	*The Alphabet War: A Story About Dyslexia* by D. Robb and D. Piazza *The Don't Give Up Kid* by J. Gehert *Thank You, Mr. Falker* by P. Polacco	*Double Dutch* by S. Draper *The Dyslexia Empowerment Plan* by B. Foss *Fish in A Tree* by L. Hunt *Hank Zipzer, The World's Greatest Underachiever: I Got a "D" in Salami* by H. Winkler and L. Oliver *Loser* by J. Spinelli
Dyscalculia	*Bump It!* by K. Sutton *This Is Not a Math Book* by A. Weltman	*Alex's Adventures in Numberland* by A. Bellos *My Thirteenth Winter* by S. Abeel *Snowflake Seashell Star* by A. Bellos
Intellectual	*Be Good to Eddie Lee* by V. Fleming *We'll Paint the Octopus Red* *Our Brother Has Down Syndrome* by S. Cairo *What's Wrong with Timmy* by M. Schriver	*The Man Who Loved Clowns* by J. Wood *The Memory Keeper's Daughter* by K. Edwards *Of Mice and Men* by J. Steinbeck *Riding the Bus with My Sister* by R. Simon *A Step Toward Falling* by C. McGovern *So B. It* by S. Weeks
Communication/Sensory	*Apartment 3* by E. Keats *El Deafo* by C. Bell *I Have a Sister My Sister Is Deaf* by J. Peterson *Knots on a Counting Rope* by B. Martin Jr. and J. Archambault *Luna and the Big Blur* by S. Day *Silent Lotus* by J. Lee *Talk to Me* by S. Brearley	*All the Light We Cannot See* by A. Doerr *Blind* by R. DeWoskin *Hurt Go Happy* by G. Rorby *A Mango-Shaped Space* by W. Mass *Miss Spitfire* by S. Miller *Of Sound Mind* by J. Ferris *Out of My Mind* by S. Draper *Singing Hands* by D. Ray

Difference	Elementary Level	Upper Elementary/Secondary Level
Physical	*Andy Finds a Turtle* by N. Holcomb *Rolling Along with Goldilocks and the Three Bears* by C. Meyers	*Annie's World* by N. Levison *The Dive from Clausen's Pier* by A. Packer *Freak the Mighty* by R. Philbrick *I Funny* by J. Patterson *Stuck in Neutral* by Terry Trueman *The View from Saturday* by E. L. Konigsburg *Wonder* by S. Draper

Appendix E

Acronyms

AAC: Alternative Augmentative Communication
AAIDD: American Association of Intellectual and Developmental Disabilities
ABA: Applied Behavior Analysis
ABC: Antecedent, Behavior, Consequence
ADA: The Americans with Disabilities Act
ADHD: Attention Deficit Hyperactivity Disorder
ADL: Activities of Daily Living
ASHA: American Speech Language Hearing Association
APA: American Psychiatric Association
APD: Auditory Processing Disorder
ASD: Autism Spectrum Disorder
ASL: American Sign Language
AT: Assistive Technology
BIP: Behavioral Intervention Plan
CAPD: Central Auditory Processing Disorder
CART: Communication Access Realtime Translation
CASEL: Collaborative for Academic, Social, and Emotional Learning
CAST: Center for Applied and Special Technology
CBA: Curriculum-Based Assessment
CDC: Centers for Disease Control and Prevention
DI: Differentiated Instruction
DOL: Daily Oral Language
DSM: Diagnostic and Statistical Manual
EBP: Evidence-Based Practice
ED: Emotional Disturbance
EHA: The Education for All Handicapped Children Act

EF: Executive Functions
ESSA: The Every Student Succeeds Act
ESY: Extended School Year
FAPE: Free and Appropriate Public Education
FBA: Functional Behavioral Assessment
GE: General Education
IIAES: Interim Alternate Education Placement
ID: Intellectual Disability
IDA: International Dyslexia Association
IDEA: Individuals with Disabilities Education Act
IEP: Individualized Education Program
IQ: Intelligence Quotient
LEA: Local Education Agency
LRE: Least Restrictive Environment
MTSS: Multitiered System of Support
OCD: Obsessive-Compulsive Disorder
OCR: Optimal Character Recognition
OCR: Office of Civil Rights
ODD: Oppositional Defiant Disorder
OHI: Other Health Impairment
OT: Occupational Therapy
PBIS: Positive Behavioral Interventions and Supports
PBL: Project-Based Learning
PLAAFP: Present Level of Academic Achievement and Functional Performance
PT: Physical Therapy
RAN: Rapid Automatic Naming
RTI: Response to Intervention
SDI: Specially Designed Instruction
SE: Special Education
SEL: Social-Emotional Learning
SGD: Speech Generating Device
SLD: Specific Learning Disability
SLP: Speech and Language Pathologist
TBI: Traumatic Brain Injury
UDL: Universal Design for Learning
WWC: What Works Clearinghouse
ZPD: Zone of Proximal Development

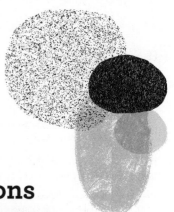

Appendix F
Professional Organizations

You are invited to explore the following organizations to discover additional knowledge about specific disabilities and interventions.

American Academy of Child and Adolescent Psychiatry: www.aacap.org

American Association of Blind Teachers: www.blindteachers.net

American Association on Intellectual and Developmental Disabilities (AAIDD): https://aaidd.org

American Foundation for the Blind: www.afb.org/default.aspx

American Psychiatric Association: www.psychiatry.org

American Speech-Language-Hearing Association: www.asha.org

Apple Accessibility: www.apple.com/accessibility/ios

Attention Deficit Disorder Association (ADDA): www.add.org

Auditory Processing Disorder Foundation: www.theapdfoundation.org

Autism Speaks: www.autismspeaks.org

Autism Theater Initiative: www.tdf.org/nyc/40/Autism-Theatre-Initiative

Bookshare: www.bookshare.org/cms

CAST (Universal Design for Learning): www.cast.org

Center for Effective and Collaborative Practices: http://cecp.air.org/promisingpractices/default.asp

Center for Effective Collaboration and Practice, Contingency Management Information for Families: http://cecp.air.org/familybriefs/docs/CONTINGENCY.pdf

Center for Parent Information and Resources: www.parentcenterhub.org

Center for Teaching Excellence, University of Virginia: http://cte.virginia.edu

Center on Brain Injury Research and Training (CBIRT): http://cbirt.org/tbi-education/executive-functions/classroom-interventions-executive-functions

Center on Technology and Disability: http://ctdinstitute.org

Centers for Disease Control and Prevention: www.cdc.gov

Childhood Apraxia of Speech Association of North America (CASANA): http://casana.pr.co

Children and Adults with Attention-Deficit/Hyperactivity Disorder (CHADD): www.chadd.org

Collaborative for Academic, Social, and Emotional Learning: www.casel.org

Collaborative for Communication Access via Captioning: http://ccacaptioning.org/faqs-cart

Colorin Colorado: www.colorincolorado.org

Deaf Child Worldwide: www.deafchildworldwide.info

Deaf-Blind Education: www.deafblindinfo.org

Depression and Bipolar Support Alliance: www.dbsalliance.org

Do2Learn Educational Resources for Special Needs: www.do2learn.com

Dyscalculia: www.dyscalculia.org

Dyslexia Buddy Network: www.dyslexiabuddynetwork.com

Educational Audiology Association: https://edaud.org

Enrichment Audio Resources Center: www.earsforeyes.info

Every Student Succeeds Act: www.ed.gov/essa?src=rn

Eye to Eye: www.eyetoeyenational.org

Gallaudet University: www.gallaudet.edu/rsia/world-deaf-information-resource/deaf-information-resources.html

Hearing Loss Association of America: www.hearingloss.org

Institute for Multisensory Education: www.orton-gillingham.com

International Dyslexia Association (IDA): http://eida.org

International OCD Foundation: https://iocdf.org/about-ocd

Intervention Central: www.interventioncentral.org

Iris Center, Vanderbilt Peabody College: http://iris.peabody.vanderbilt.edu

Kennedy Center, VSA, The International Organization on Arts and Disability: http://education.kennedy-center.org//education/vsa

Knowledge and Practice Standards for Teachers of Reading: https://eida.org/kps-for-teachers-of-reading

LD Online: www.ldonline.org

Learning Disabilities Association of America: www.ldanatl.org

Listening and Spoken Language Knowledge Center: www.agbell.org

Mental Health America: www.nmha.org

National Alliance of Blind Students: www.blindstudents.org

National Alliance on Mental Illness: www.nami.org

National Center for Learning Disabilities (NCLD): http://ncld.org

National Center on Universal Design for Learning: www.udlcenter.org/aboutudl/udlguidelines

National Coalition of Auditory Processing: www.ncapd.org/What_is_APD_.html

National Council of Teachers of English: www.ncte.org

National Council of Teachers of Mathematics: www.nctm.org

National Down Syndrome Society: www.ndss.org/Down-Syndrome/What-Is-Down-Syndrome

National Federation of Families for Children's Mental Health: www.ffcmh.org

National Federation of the Blind: https://nfb.org

National Institute of Mental Health: www.nimh.nih.gov/index.shtml

National Organization on Fetal Alcohol Syndrome: www.nofas.org

National Professional Development Center on Autism Spectrum Disorder: http://autismpdc.fpg.unc.edu

National Technical Assistance Center on Positive Behavioral Interventions and Supports: www.pbis.org

Office of Special Education and Rehabilitative Services (OSERS): www2.ed.gov/about/offices/list/osers/osep/index.html

PACER Center: Champions for Children with Disabilities: www.pacer.org

Paths to Literacy: www.pathstoliteracy.org/technology-students-multiple-disabilities

PE Central–Adaptive Physical Education Resources: www.pecentral.org/adapted/adaptedmenu.html

Readworks: www.readworks.org

ReadWriteThink: www.readwritethink.org

RTI Action Network: www.rtinetwork.org/learn/researchuse-rti-identify-students-learning-disabilities-review-research

Selective Mutism Anxiety Research and Treatment Center: www.selectivemutismcenter.org/aboutus/whatisselectivemutism

State of New Jersey Department of Education: www.state.nj.us/education/specialed/dyslexia/pd.shtml

Strategic Instruction Model, The University of Kansas: http://sim.kucrl.org

Teaching LD: www.dldcec.org

Teaching Tolerance: www.tolerance.org

Temple University Institute on Disabilities: www.temple.edu/instituteondisabilities

The Arc: For People with Intellectual and Developmental Disabilities: www.thearc.org

The Center for Neurological and Neurodevelopment Health: www.cnnh.org

Think College! College Options for People with Intellectual Disabilities: www.thinkcollege.net

U.S. National Library of Medicine–Medline Plus: https://medlineplus.gov/?utm_source=www.domtail
.com

Understanding Dysgraphia: www.understood.org/en/learning-attention-issues/
child-learning-disabilities/dysgraphia/understanding-dysgraphia

Understood for Learning and Attention Issues: www.understood.org/en

United Cerebral Palsy: http://ucp.org

University of Kansas Center for Research on Learning: Learning Strategies: www.ku-crl.org/sim/
strategies.shtml

University of Michigan: http://dyslexiahelp.umich.edu/dyslexics/learn-about-dyslexia/dyslexia-testing/
tests

Web MD Autism Topic Overview: www.webmd.com/brain/autism/autism-topic-overview

YAI, Seeing Beyond Disability: www.yai.org

Yale Center for Dyslexia and Creativity: http://dyslexia.yale.edu

Index

The letter *f* following a page number denotes a figure.

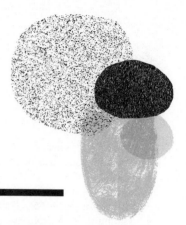

About the Author

Toby Karten—a staff developer, instructional coach, educational consultant, author, adjunct professor, and inclusion specialist—has taught populations of learners at levels ranging from preschool to graduate school. She has collaborated with administrators, staff, students, and their families at local, national, and international school sites and educational conferences as an invited speaker and inclusion coach. She has an undergraduate degree in special education from Brooklyn College, a master's degree in special education from the College of Staten Island, a supervisory degree from Georgian Court University, and an honorary doctorate from Gratz College. Ms. Karten has been recognized by the Council for Exceptional Children and the New Jersey Department of Education as an exemplary educator, receiving two Teacher of the Year awards. She has instructed learners across every setting in the continuum representing the least restrictive environment. Her ongoing professional goal is to help learners achieve successful inclusion experiences in school and life.